D1094392

GRANNIES

GRANNIES

SIXTH&SPRING BOOKS
NEW YORK

SIXTH&SPRING BOOKS
233 Spring Street
New York, New York 10013

Library of Congress Control Number: 2008925016

ISBN-10: 1-933027-66-5
ISBN-13: 978-1-933027-66-1

Manufactured in China

1 3 5 7 9 10 8 6 4 2

First Edition, 2008

TABLE OF CONTENTS

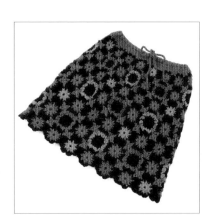

INTRODUCTION

It's hip to be square! *Grannies* takes granny squares out of the afghan (although we do have a couple of those!) and transforms them into a gorgeous collection of apparel and home décor projects.

Grannies are incredibly versatile. You can turn a single granny into a stylish ring, whip up a simple tote by joining two large grannies, piece together multiple small squares to create a patchwork baby blanket, or trim a chic capelet with a border of grannies. There's no limit to the possible combinations.

The styles in this inspirational book range from classic and timeless to fun and funky and feature a variety of beautiful yarns made from traditional fibers such as merino wool, cotton and mohair to more unusual fibers such as ribbon, camel and bamboo. Less experienced crocheters as well as those looking for a challenge will find tons of projects to choose from, including a lacy cropped cardigan, stunning throw pillows, a cozy scarf, a groovy circular handbag, a fabulous drawstring skirt, an elegant metallic clutch, an eye-catching pendant and much more.

Whether you're new to the world of grannies or an expert looking for fresh inspiration, you'll find plenty of designs to sink your hook into. So grab your yarn and your hook and get ready to crochet **ON THE GO!**

THE BASICS

As you will see from the variety of projects in this book, grannies are extremely versatile. You can use grannies on their own, combine them with other grannies, or embellish a piece with grannies. The design possibilities are endless.

A granny square is worked in rounds, meaning that you start in the middle and your piece gets larger as you add rounds. You can easily adjust the size of a granny by adding or omitting rounds, making it easy to customize projects to your needs and taste. The designs in this book range from quick and easy to more complex and from traditional to fashion-forward to entice every crocheter.

YARN SELECTION

For an exact reproduction of the photographed project, use the yarn listed in the materials section of the pattern. We've selected yarns that are readily available in the U.S. and Canada at the time of printing. The Resources list on pages 94 and 95 provides addresses of yarn distributors. Contact them for the name of a retailer in your area.

YARN SUBSTITUTION

You may wish to substitute yarns. Perhaps you view small-scale projects as a chance to incorporate leftovers from your yarn stash, or maybe the yarn specified is not available in your area. You'll need to crochet to the given gauge to obtain the finished measurements with the substitute yarn (see "Gauge" on page 11). Make pattern adjustments where necessary. Be sure to consider how different yarn types (chenille, mohair, bouclé, etc.) will affect the final appearance and feel of your project. Also take fiber care into consideration: Some yarns can be machine- or hand-washed; others will require dry cleaning.

To facilitate yarn substitution, this book gives the standard yarn weight for each yarn. You'll find a yarn weight symbol in the "Materials" section of the pattern, immediately following the yarn information. Look for a substitute yarn that falls into the same category. The suggested hook size and gauge on the ball band should be comparable to those on the Standard Yarn Weight System chart on page 13.

After you've successfully gauge-swatched a substitute yarn, you'll need to determine how much of the substitute yarn the project requires. First, find the total yardage of the original yarn in the pattern (multiply the number of balls by yards/meters per ball). Divide this figure by the new yards/meters per ball (listed on the ball band). Round up to the next whole number. The result is the number of balls required.

GAUGE

Most of the patterns in this book don't rely on perfect fit, but it is still important to crochet a gauge swatch. Measure gauge as illustrated here. (Launder and block your gauge swatch before taking measurements). Try different hook sizes until your sample measures the required number of stitches and rows. To get fewer stitches to the inch/cm, use a larger hook; to get more stitches to the inch/cm, use a smaller hook. It's a good idea to keep your gauge swatch to test embroidery, embellishments or blocking and cleaning methods.

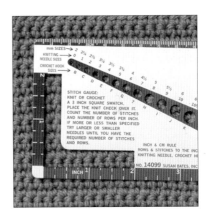

CROCHET HOOKS

U.S.	Metric	U.S.	Metric	U.S.	Metric
B/1	2.25mm	G/6	4mm	K/10.5	6.5mm
C/2	2.75mm	7	4.5mm	L/11	8mm
D/3	3.25mm	H/8	5mm	M/13	9mm
E/4	3.5mm	I/9	5.5mm	N/15	10mm
F/5	3.75mm	J/10	6mm		

READING CROCHET INSTRUCTIONS

If you are used to reading knitting instructions, then crochet instructions may seem a little tedious to follow. Crochet instructions use more abbreviations and punctuation and fewer words than traditional knitting instructions. Along with the separation of stitches and use of brackets, parentheses, commas and other punctuation, numerous repetitions may occur within a single row or round. Therefore, you must pay close attention to reading instructions while you crochet. Here are a few explanations of the more common terms used in this book.

Use of Parentheses ( )

Sometimes parentheses are used to indicate stitches that are to be worked all into one stitch such as "in next st work ( )" or "( ) in next st."

First st, Next st

The beginning stitch of every row is referred to as the "first st." When counting the turning chain (t-ch) as one stitch, the row or round will begin by instructing that you work into the next st (that is, skip the first st or space or whatever is designated in the pattern).

Stitch Counts

Sometimes the turning chain that is worked at the end (or beginning) of a row or a round will be referred to as 1 stitch, and it is then counted in the stitch count. In those cases, you will work into the next stitch, thus skipping the first stitch of the row or round. When the turning chain is not counted as a stitch, work into the first actual stitch.

Stitches Described

Sometimes the stitches are described as sc, dc, tr, ch-2 loop, 2-dc group, etc., and sometimes—

such as in a mesh pattern of sc, ch 1—each sc and each ch 1 will be referred to as a st.

Back Loop, Front Loop

Along the top of each crochet stitch or chain there are two loops. The loop farthest away from you is the "back loop." The loop closest to you is the "front loop."

Joining New Colors

When joining new colors in crochet, whether at the beginning of a row or while working across, always work the stitch in the old color to the last 2 loops, then draw the new color through the 2 loops and continue with the new color.

Working Over Ends

Crochet has a unique flat top along each row that is perfect for laying the old color across and working over the ends for several stitches. This will alleviate the need to cut and weave in ends later.

Making a Ring

When a pattern is worked in the round, as in a square or granny, the beginning chains are usually closed into a ring by working a slip stitch into the first chain. Then on the first round, stitches are usually worked into the ring and less often into each chain. (See photos on page 14.)

BLOCKING

Blocking crochet is usually not necessary. However, in those cases when you do need to smooth out the fabric, choose a blocking method consistent with information on the yarn care label and, when in doubt, test your gauge

Categories of yarn, gauge ranges, and recommended needle and hook sizes

Yarn Weight Symbol & Category Names	**1** Super Fine	**2** Fine	**3** Light	**4** Medium	**5** Bulky	**6** Super Bulky
Type of Yarns in Category	Sock, Fingering, Baby	Sport, Baby	DK, Light Worsted	Worsted, Afghan, Aran	Chunky, Craft, Rug	Bulky, Roving
Knit Gauge Range* in Stockinette Stitch to 4 Inches	27–32 sts	23–26 sts	21–24 sts	16–20 sts	12–15 sts	6–11 sts
Recommended Needle in Metric Size Range	2.25–3.25 mm	3.25–3.75 mm	3.75–4.5 mm	4.5–5.5 mm	5.5–8 mm	8 mm and larger
Recommended Needle in U.S. Size Range	1 to 3	3 to 5	5 to 7	7 to 9	9 to 11	11 and larger
Crochet Gauge* Range in Single Crochet to 4 Inches	21–32 sts	16–20 sts	12–17 sts	11–14 sts	8–11 sts	5–9 sts
Recommended Hook in Metric Size Range	2.25–3.5 mm	3.5–4.5 mm	4.5 5.5 mm	5.5–6.5 mm	6.5–9 mm	9 mm and larger
Recommended Hook in U.S. Size Range	B-1 to E-4	E-4 to 7	7 to I-9	I-9 to K-10.5	K-10.5 to M-13	M-13 and larger

*Guidelines only: The above reflects the most commonly used needle or hook sizes for specific yarn categories.

Beginner
Ideal first project.

Easy
Basic stitches, minimal shaping, simple finishing.

Intermediate
For crocheters with some experience. More intricate stitches, shaping and finishing.

Experienced
For crocheters able to work patterns with complicated shaping and finishing.

swatch. Note that some yarns, such as chenilles and ribbons, do not benefit from blocking.

Wet Block Method

Using rustproof pins, pin the piece to measurements on a flat surface and lightly dampen using a spray bottle. Allow to dry before removing pins.

Steam Block Method

Pin the piece to measurements with wrong side of the fabric facing up. Steam lightly, holding the iron 2"/5cm above the work. Do not press the iron directly onto the piece, as it will flatten the stitches.

CARE

Refer to the yarn label for the recommended cleaning method. Many of the projectss in the book can be washed by hand (or in the machine on a gentle or wool cycle) in lukewarm water with a mild detergent. Do not agitate, and don't soak for more than 10 minutes. Rinse gently with tepid water, then fold in a towel and gently press the water out. Lay flat to dry, away from excessive heat and light.

MAKING A RING

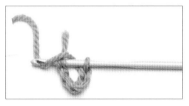

1 To make a practice ring, chain six. Insert the hook through both loops of the first chain stitch made. Yarn over and draw through the chain stitch and the loop on the hook in one movement.

2 You have now joined the chain with a slip stitch and formed a ring.

1 Chain five. Join the chain with a slip stitch, forming a ring. Chain three (equals the height of a double crochet stitch). Work twelve double crochets in the ring, then join the round with a slip stitch in the top two loops of the first stitch.

The whipstitch is used for joining granny squares as well as other short, straight edges. Thread the tail from the foundation chain through a yarn needle. Place the pieces together so the wrong sides are facing, edges are even and stitches line up. Insert the needle into the back loop of the piece in front and into the front loop of the adjacent stitch of the piece in back. Continue to work in this manner, drawing the yarn only tight enough to keep the edges together.

2 For the second round, chain three. Work two double crochet in each of the twelve stitches. Join the round with a slip stitch in the first stitch you now have twenty-four stitches. To practice one more round, chain three, *work one double crochet in the next stitch, then work two double crochet in the following stitch. Repeat from the * to the end of the round. Join the round with a slip stitch in the first stitch you now have thirty-six stitches.

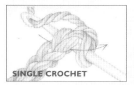

CHAIN

1 *Pass the yarn over the hook and catch it with the hook.*

2 *Draw the yarn through the loop on the hook.*

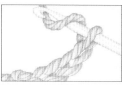

3 *Repeat steps 1 and 2 to make a chain.*

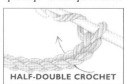

SINGLE CROCHET

1 *Insert the hook through top two loops of a stitch. Pass the yarn over the hook and draw up a loop—two loops on hook.*

2 *Pass the yarn over the hook and draw through both loops on hook.*

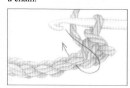

3 *Continue in the same way, inserting the hook into each stitch.*

HALF-DOUBLE CROCHET

1 *Pass the yarn over the hook. Insert the hook through the top two loops of a stitch.*

2 *Pass the yarn over the hook and draw up a loop—three loops on hook. Pass the yarn over the hook.*

3 *Draw through all three loops on hook.*

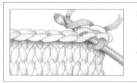

DOUBLE CROCHET

1 *Pass the yarn over the hook. Insert the hook through the top two loops of a stitch.*

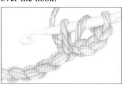

2 *Pass the yarn over the hook and draw up a loop—three loops on hook.*

SLIP STITCH

Insert the crochet hook into a stitch, catch the yarn and pull up a loop. Draw the loop through the loop on the hook.

3 *Pass the yarn over the hook and draw it through the first two loops on the hook, pass the yarn over the hook and draw through the remaining two loops. Continue in the same way, inserting the hook into each stitch.*

Illustrations: Joni Coniglio

CROCHET TERMS AND ABBREVIATIONS

approx approximately

beg begin(ning)

CC contrast color

ch chain(s)

cm centimeter(s)

cont continue(ing)

dc double crochet (UK: tr—treble)

dec decrease(ing)—reduce the stitches in a row (work stitches together or skip the stitches)

foll follow(s)(ing)

g gram(s)

hdc half double crochet (UK: htr—half treble)

inc increase(ing)—add stitches in a row (work extra stitches into a stitch or between the stitches)

LH left-hand

lp(s) loop(s)

m meter(s)

MC main color

mm millimeter(s)

oz ounce(s)

pat(s) pattern

pm place markers—place or attach a loop of contrast yarn or purchased stitch marker

as indicated

rem remain(s)(ing)

rep repeat

rnd(s) round(s)

RH right-hand

RS right side(s)

sc single crochet (UK: dc—double crochet)

sk skip

sl st slip stitch (UK: single crochet)

sp(s) space(s)

st(s) stitch(es)

t-ch turning chain

tog together

tr treble (UK: tr tr—triple treble)

WS wrong side(s)

work even continue in pattern without increasing or decreasing (UK: work straight)

yd yard(s)

yo yarn over—wrap the yarn around the hook (UK: yrh)

* = repeat directions following * as many times as indicated

[ ] = repeat directions inside brackets as many times as indicated

PONCHO
Fiesta!

You can wear this generously sized half-granny a number of ways. When laced up with its tassel tie, it has poncho punch. Without the tie, it's a sensational shawl. Designed by Marty Miller.

SIZES
Instructions are written for one size.

FINISHED MEASUREMENTS
▨ Approx 66"/167.5cm wide x 34"/86.5cm long

MATERIALS
▨ 3 3½oz/100g hanks (each approx 157yd/144m) of Colinette/Unique Kolours *Giotto* (cotton/rayon/nylon) in #102 pierro
▨ Sizes K/10.5 and N/15 (6.5 and 10mm) crochet hooks *or sizes to obtain gauge*

GAUGE
12 sts and 4¼ rows to 4"/10cm in pat st using larger crochet hook.
Take time to check gauge.

SHAWL
Beg at top edge (center neck edge), with larger hook, ch 4. Join ch with a sl st, forming a ring. Turn.
Row I (RS) Ch 4 (always counts as 1 dc and ch 1), [3 dc in ring, ch 1] twice, dc in ring—8 dc and 3 ch-1 sps. Turn.
Row 2 Ch 4, (3 dc, ch 1) in first ch-1 sp, [3 dc, ch 1] twice in next ch-1 sp—corner

made, (3 dc, ch 1) in next ch-1 sp, dc in same ch-1 sp—14 dc and 5 ch-1 sps. Turn.
Row 3 Ch 4, (3 dc, ch 1) in first ch-1 sp, (3 dc , ch 1) in next ch-1 sp, [3 dc, ch 1] twice in corner ch-1 sp, (3 dc, ch 1) in next ch-1 sp, (3 dc, ch 1) in last ch-1 sp, dc in same ch-1 sp—20 dc and 7 ch-1 sps. Turn.
Row 4 Ch 4, (3 dc, ch 1) in each ch-1 sp to corner, [3 dc, ch 1] twice in corner ch-1 sp, (3 dc, ch 1) in each ch-1 sp to last ch-1 sp, (3 dc, ch 1) in last ch-1 sp, dc in same ch-1 sp—26 dc and 9 ch-1 sps. Turn.
Rows 5–24 Rep row 4—146 dc and 49 ch-1 sps. Turn to side edge.

Edging
Row I Ch 1, making sure that work lies flat, sc evenly across entire top edge. Fasten off.

TIE
Make a slipknot, leaving a 12"/30.5cm tail. Place slipknot on smaller hook, then ch 150. Fasten off, leaving a 12"/30.5cm tail. For each end of tie, cut four 20"/51cm lengths of yarn. Gather strands tog with ends even. Fold strands in half. Insert hook through last ch and through folded yarn. Pull folded yarn through, then draw ends and tail through fold and tighten. Rep for opposite end of ch. Trim ends even. Fold top edge of shawl in half with edges even. Beg at row 14, lace tie along top edge, like a shoelace, to row 8.

TASSELED HAT

Snow-capped

A ring of little squares forms the foundation for this wonderful winter hat. The striped crown and braided tassels make it extra-special. Designed by Jacqueline Jewett.

SIZES
Instructions are written for one size.

FINISHED MEASUREMENTS
- Head circumference 21"/53.5cm
- Depth 9"/23cm

MATERIALS
- 1 1¾oz/50g skein (approx 109yd/100m) of Knit One, Crochet Too, Inc. *Camelino* (merino wool/camel) each in #695 marine blue (A), #620 ice (B), #557 pine (C), #527 celery (D), #510 silver sage (E) and #629 steel (F) **(4)**
- Size F/5 and K/10.5 (3.75 and 6.5mm) crochet hooks *or size to obtain gauges*

GAUGES
- 20 sts and 10½ rnds to 4"/10cm over dc using smaller crochet hook.
- One motif is 3½"/9cm square using smaller crochet hook.
Take time to check gauges.

Notes
1 To join yarn with a sc, make a slipknot and place on hook. Insert hook in lp in st, yo, draw up a lp, yo and draw through both lps on hook.

2 When changing colors, draw new color through last 2 lps on hook when completing st and carry unused color behind work.

3 Joining of rounds is in top of beg ch-3 throughout.

STITCH GLOSSARY
BL (bobble st) In same st [yo, insert hook into st, yo and draw up a lp, yo and draw through 2 lps on hook] 3 times, yo and draw through all 4 lps on hook.

CROWN
With smaller hook and A, ch 6. Join ch with a sl st, forming a ring.

Rnd 1 (RS) Ch 1, 12 sc in ring, join rnd with a sl st in first sc.

Rnd 2 Ch 3 (always count as 1 dc), dc in same ch-3 sp, 2 dc in st around, join rnd with a sl st in first dc—18 sts. Fasten off. Turn.

Rnd 3 (WS) Join B with a sl st in same st as joining of rnd below, ch 3, dc in next 2 sts, *dc in next st, 2 dc in next 2 sts; rep from * around, join rnd with a sl st in first dc—30 sts. Fasten off. Turn.

Rnd 4 (RS) Join C with a sl st in same st as joining of rnd below, ch 3, 2 dc in next st, *dc in next st, 2 dc in next st; rep from * around, join rnd with a sl st in first dc—45 sts. Turn.

Rnd 5 Ch 3, dc in next 3 sts, 2 dc in next st, dc in next 4 sts, 2 dc in next st; rep from * around, join rnd with a sl st in first dc—54 sts. Fasten off. Turn.

Rnd 6 (RS) Join D with a sl st in same st as joining of rnd below, ch 3, dc in next 4 sts, 2 dc in next st, *dc in next 5 sts, 2 dc in next st; rep from * around, join rnd with a sl st in first dc—63 sts. Fasten off. Turn.

Rnd 7 (WS) Join A with a sl st in same st as joining of rnd below, ch 3, dc in next 5 sts, 2 dc in next st, *dc in next 6 sts, 2 dc in next st; rep from * around, join rnd with a sl st in first dc—72 sts. Fasten off. Turn.

Rnd 8 (RS) Join E with a sl st in same st as joining of rnd below, ch 3, dc in next 4 sts, 2 dc in next st, *dc in next 5 sts, 2 dc in next st; rep from * around, join rnd with a sl st in first dc—84 sts. Fasten off. Turn.

Rnd 9 (WS) Join F with a sl st in same st as joining of rnd below, ch 3, dc in next 5 sts, 2 dc in next st, dc in next 6 sts, 2 dc in next st; rep from * around, join rnd with a sl st in first dc—96 sts. Turn.

Rnd 10 Ch 3, dc in next 14 sts, 2 dc in next st, *dc in next 15 sts, 2 dc in next st; rep from * around, join rnd with a sl st in first dc—102 sts. Fasten off. Turn.

Rnd 11 (WS) Join D with a sl st in same st as joining of rnd below, ch 3, dc in each st around, join rnd with a sl st in first dc. Fasten off. Turn.

Rnd 12 (RS) Join C with a sl st in same st as joining of rnd below, ch 3, dc in each st around, join rnd with a sl st in first dc. Fasten off. Turn.

Rnd 13 (RS) Join A with a sl st in same st as joining of rnd below, ch 3, dc in each st around, join rnd with a sl st in first dc. Fasten off.

MOTIF I

With smaller hook and A, ch 4. Join ch with a sl st, forming a ring.

Rnd 1 (RS) Ch 3 (always counts as 1 dc), 2 dc in ring, ch 2, *3 dc in ring, ch 2; rep from * around twice more, join rnd with a sl st in top of beg ch-3—4 ch-2 sps. Fasten off. Turn.

Rnd 2 (WS) Join E with a sl st in any ch-2 sp, ch 3, in same ch-sp (dc, ch 2, 2 dc)—beg corner made, dc in next 3 sts, *(2 dc, ch 2, 2 dc) in next ch-2 sp, dc in next 3 sts; rep from * around twice more, join rnd with a sl st in top of beg ch-3—4 corner ch-2 sps. Fasten off. Turn.

Rnd 3 (RS) Join F with a sl st in any ch-2 sp, ch 3, in same ch-sp (dc, ch 2, 2 dc), dc in next 7 sts, *(2 dc, ch 2, 2 dc) in next ch-2 sp, dc in next 7 sts; rep from * around twice more, join rnd with a sl st in top of beg ch-3. Fasten off. Turn.

Rnd 4 (WS) Join B with a sl st in any ch-2 sp, ch 3, in same ch-sp (dc, ch 2, 2 dc), dc in next 11 sts, *(2 dc, ch 2, 2 dc) in next ch-2 sp, dc in next 11 sts; rep from * around twice more, join rnd with a sl st in top of beg ch-3. Fasten off leaving a long end for sewing.

MOTIF 2

With smaller hook and D, ch 4. Join ch with a sl st, forming a ring. Cont to work as motif 1 in color sequence as foll: **Rnd 1** D. **Rnd 2** C. **Rnd 3** E. **Rnd 4** A.

MOTIF 3

With smaller hook and C, ch 4. Join ch with a sl st, forming a ring. Cont to work as motif 1 in color sequence as foll: **Rnd 1** C. **Rnd 2** B. **Rnd 3** A. **Rnd 4** D.

MOTIF 4

With smaller hook and E, ch 4. Join ch with a sl st, forming a ring. Cont to work as motif 1 in color sequence as foll: **Rnd 1** E. **Rnd 2** A. **Rnd 3** B. **Rnd 4** F.

MOTIF 5

With smaller hook and F, ch 4. Join ch with a sl st, forming a ring. Cont to work as motif 1 in color sequence as foll: **Rnd 1** F. **Rnd 2** D. **Rnd 3** C. **Rnd 4** E.

MOTIF 6

With smaller hook and B, ch 4. Join ch with a sl st, forming a ring. Cont to work as motif 1 in color sequence as foll: **Rnd 1** B. **Rnd 2** A. **Rnd 3** D. **Rnd 4** C.

FINISHING

Arrange motifs in a strip as foll: 1, 2, 3, 4, 5, 6. With WS tog and working through back lps, use yarn ends to whipstitch squares tog in a strip, then whipstitch strip tog forming the hatband. Position joining seam of crown over seam of motifs 5 and 6, then using B, whipstitch bottom edge of crown to hatband.

Bottom band

With RS of hatband facing and smaller hook, join A with a sl st in seam of motifs 5 and 6.

Rnd 1 (RS) Ch 1, 90 sc evenly spaced around entire bottom edge, join rnd with a sl st in first sc. Turn.

Rnd 2 (WS) Ch1, sc in first and in each sc around, join rnd with a sl st in first sc. Turn.

Rnd 3 Ch 3, dc in next 3 sts, *with D, BL in next st, *with A*, dc in next 4 sts; rep from * around, end with D, BL in next st, join rnd with a sl st in first st. Turn.

Rnd 4 Ch 1, sc in each st around, join rnd with a sl st in first st. Turn.

Rnd 5 (RS) Ch 1, *working from left to right*, sc in each st around, join rnd with a sl st in first st. Fasten off.

Braids

For each braid cut two 36"/91.5cm strands of each color. Gather strands tog, ends even. Fold strands in half. On WS, insert larger hook from front to back between 2 dc through bottom band (above seam of motifs 1 and 6). Pull folded yarn through, then draw ends through fold and tighten. Divide strands into 3 equals bundles and braid for 3½"/9cm. Tie ends in a overhand knot. Rep for opposite side of hat, positioning braid above seam of motifs 3 and 4.

Grannies get the royal treatment when worked in regal jewel tones. Amy Polcyn used different color combinations to get maximum eye appeal for this warm and woolly scarf.

FINISHED MEASUREMENTS
■ Approx 5½"/14cm wide x 66"/167.5cm long

MATERIALS
■ 1 1¾oz/50g skein (approx 93yd/85m) of Nashua Handknits/Westminster Fibers, Inc. *Julia* (wool/alpaca/mohair) each in #3961 ladies mantle (A), #2083 magenta (B), #9235 anemone (C), #1220 tarnished brass (D) and #3158 purple basil (E) ❹
■ Size H/8 (5mm) crochet hook *or size to obtain gauge*

GAUGE
One motif is 5½"/14cm square using size H/8 (5mm) crochet hook.
Take time to check gauge.

MOTIF 1 (MAKE 3)
With A, ch 4. Join ch with a sl st, forming a ring.
Rnd 1 (RS) Ch 3 (always counts as 1 dc), 2 dc in ring, ch 1, * 3 dc in ring, ch 1; rep from * around twice more, join rnd with a sl st in top of beg ch-3—4 ch-1 sps. Fasten off.
Rnd 2 (RS) Join B with a sl st in any ch-1 sp, ch 3, in same ch-sp work (2 dc, ch 1, 3

dc—beg corner made), ch 1, *(3 dc, ch 1, 3 dc) in next ch-1 sp, ch 1; rep from * around twice more, join rnd with a sl st in top of beg ch-3—4 corner ch-1 sps. Fasten off.

Rnd 3 (RS) Join C with a sl st in any corner ch-1 sp, ch 3, in same ch-sp work (2 dc, ch 1, 3 dc), ch 1, 3 dc in next ch-1 sp, ch 1, *(3 dc, ch 1, 3 dc) in next corner ch-1 sp, ch 1, 3 dc in next ch-1 sp, ch 1; rep from * around twice more, join rnd with a sl st in top of beg ch-3. Fasten off.

Rnd 4 (RS) Join D with a sl st in any corner ch-1 sp, ch 3, in same ch-sp work (2 dc, ch 1, 3 dc), ch 1, [3 dc in next ch-1 sp, ch 1] twice, *(3 dc, ch 1, 3 dc) in next corner ch-1 sp, ch 1, [3 dc in next ch-1 sp, ch 1] twice; rep from * around twice more, join rnd with a sl st in top of beg ch-3. Fasten off.

Rnd 5 (RS) Join E with a sl st in any corner ch-1 sp, ch 3, in same ch-sp work (2 dc, ch 1, 3 dc), ch 1, [3 dc in next ch-1 sp, ch 1] 3 times, *(3 dc, ch 1, 3 dc) in next corner ch-1 sp, ch 1, [3 dc in next ch-1 sp, ch 1] 3 times; rep from * around twice more, join rnd with a sl st in top of beg ch-3. Fasten off, leaving long tail for sewing.

MOTIF 2 (MAKE 3)
With C, ch 4. Join ch with a sl st, forming a ring. Cont to work as motif 1 in color sequence as foll: **Rnd 1** C. **Rnd 2** D. **Rnd 3** A. **Rnd 4** B. **Rnd 5** E.

With B, ch 4. Join ch with a sl st, forming a ring. Cont to work as motif 1 in color sequence as foll: **Rnd 1** B. **Rnd 2** C. **Rnd 3** D. **Rnd 4** A. **Rnd 5** E.

With D, ch 4. Join ch with a sl st, forming a ring. Cont to work as motif 1 in color sequence as foll: **Rnd 1** D. **Rnd 2** A. **Rnd 3** B. **Rnd 4** C. **Rnd 5** E.

Arrange motifs in a strip as foll: 1, 2, 3, 4, 1, 2, 3, 4, 1, 2, 3, 4. With WS tog and working through back lps, use yarn ends to whip-stitch squares tog.

DRAWSTRING SKIRT

Stitchwork orange

It's that 70's style that's all the rage once more. Designer Gayle Bunn has embraced the best of the past with this fabulous skirt crocheted in earthy autumnal tones.

SIZES

Instructions are written for size Small/Medium.

FINISHED MEASUREMENTS

- Lower edge 56"/142cm
- Waist 36"/91.5cm
- Length 25"/63.5cm

MATERIALS

- 3 3oz/85g skeins (each approx 197yd/180m) of Lion Brand Yarn *Wool-Ease* (acrylic/wool) each in #188 paprika and #126 chocolate brown (4)
- 1 skein each in #129 cocoa and #174 avocado
- Size H/8 and I/9 (5 and 5.5mm) crochet hooks *or sizes to obtain gauges*

GAUGES

- Large motif to 3½"/9cm square using larger crochet hook.
- Small motif to 3"/7.5cm square using smaller crochet hook.

Take time to check gauges.

Notes

1 To join yarn with a sc, make a slipknot and place on hook. Insert hook in st, yo, draw up a lp, yo and draw through both lps on hook.

2 Skirt is made of 7 horizontal strips of 16 motifs each. Referring to diagram and following it from *left to right*, work the 4–motif rep 4 times across for each strip.

3 Use larger hook to make strips 1–4 for bottom of skirt, then use smaller hook to rep strips 1–3 for top of skirt.

STITCH GLOSSARY

CL (cluster st) In same sp [yo, insert hook into ring, yo and draw up a lp, yo and draw through 2 lps on hook] 3 times, yo and draw through all 4 lps on hook.

dc2tog In same sp [yo, insert hook into ring, yo and draw up a lp, yo and draw through 2 lps on hook] twice, yo and draw through all 3 lps on hook.

SKIRT

First motif

With larger hook and paprika, ch 6. Join ch with a sl st forming a ring.

Rnd 1 (RS) Ch 3 (counts as 1 dc), dc2tog in ring (beg CL made), ch 3, [CL in ring, ch 3] 7 times, join rnd with a sl st in top of beg CL—8 CL sts. Fasten off.

Rnd 2 (RS) Join chocolate brown with a sc in top of any CL st, ch 3, CL in next ch-3 sp, ch 3, [sc in top of next CL, ch 3, CL in next ch-3 sp, ch 3] 7 times, join rnd with a sl st in first sc. Fasten off.

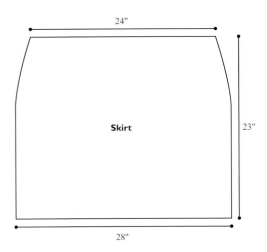

24"

Skirt

23"

28"

Making and joining second motif

With larger hook and cocoa, ch 6. Join ch with a sl st, forming a ring.

Rnd 1 (RS) Rep rnd 1 as for first motif.

Rnd 2 (joining) With RS facing, join chocolate brown with a sc in top of any CL st, ch 3, CL in next ch-3 sp, ch 3, sc in top of next CL, ch 3, CL in next ch-3 sp, sl st in corresponding CL of first motif, ch 3, sc in top of next CL of 2nd motif, ch 3, CL in next ch-3 sp of 2nd motif, sl st in corresponding CL of first motif, ch 3, cont around 2nd motif as foll: [sc in top of next CL, ch 3, CL in next ch-3 sp, ch3] 5 times, join rnd with a sl st in first sc. Fasten off.

Making and joining next 14 motifs

Cont to join motifs as for 2nd motif until 15 motifs are joined. Make and join the 16th motif to the 15th motif and then the first motif, forming a circle.

Making and joining rem motifs

Cont to work in the same manner, joining motifs on rnd 2 to each corresponding CL st with a sl st and joining last 2 motifs to cont the circle.

FILLER MOTIFS

Use larger hook for bottom 4 strips and smaller hook for top 3 strips.

With paprika, ch 4. Join ch with a sl st, forming a ring.

Rnd 1 (RS) *Ch 3, sl st in matching sc of adjoining motif, ch 3, sc in ring; rep from * 3 times more. Fasten off.

FINISHING
Lightly block to measurements.

Waistband
Rnd 1 (RS) With smaller hook, join paprika with sl st in sc between top 2 clusters of any square at top edge, ch 5 (counts 1 hdc and ch 3), *sc in top of next CL, dc2tog in next sc of same motif, dc2tog in opposite sc of next adjoining motif, sc in top of next CL, ch 3**, hdc in next sc, ch 3; rep from * around, end last rep at **, join rnd with a sl st in 2nd ch of beg ch-5.

Rnd 2 Ch 1, sc in same space with joining, *2 sc in next ch-3 sp, sc in next sc, [sc in next dc2tog] twice, sc in next sc, 2 sc in next ch-3 sp, sc in next hdc; rep from * around, end last rep with 2 sc in last ch-3 sp, join rnd with a sl st in first sc.

Rnds 3–5 Ch 3 (counts as 1 dc), dc in each st around, join rnd with a sl st to top of beg ch-3. When rnd 5 is completed, fasten off.

Drawstring
With larger hook and 2 strands of paprika held tog, ch for 76"/193cm. Fasten off. Beg and ending at center front, weave drawstring over and under every 2 dc around. Knot ends of drawstring.

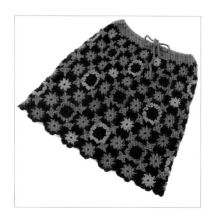

Assembly Diagram

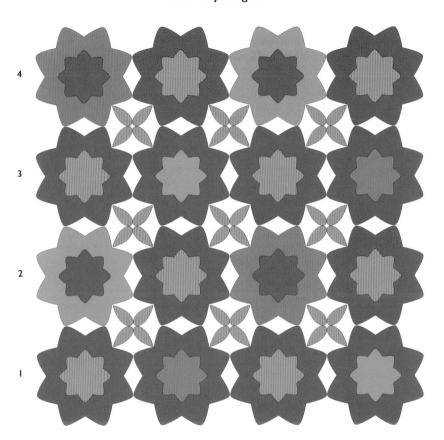

COLOR KEY

- ■ Chocolate brown
- ▨ Paprika
- ■ Avocado
- ■ Cocoa

It's as easy as child's play to crochet this **adorable pint-size patchwork afghan. Small fry will love the vivid colors and its comfy hugability. Designed by Marilyn Losee.**

FINISHED MEASUREMENTS

■ Approx 32"/81cm wide x 36"/91.5cm long

MATERIALS

■ 2 6oz/170g skeins (each approx 315yd/288m) of Caron International *Simply Soft Brites* (acrylic) in #9602 off white (MC)

■ 1 skein each in #9604 watermelon (A), #9605 mango (B), #9606 lemonade (C), #9607 limelight (D), #9608 blue mint (E) and #9610 grape (F)

■ Size G/6 (4mm) crochet hook *or size to obtain gauge*

GAUGE

One motif to 5"/12.5cm square using size G/6 (4mm) crochet hook.
Take time to check gauge.

Note

To join yarn with a sc, make a slipknot and place on hook. Insert hook in st, yo, draw up a lp, yo and draw through both lps on hook.

MOTIF A (MAKE 5)

With A, ch 6. Join ch with a sl st, forming a ring.

Rnd 1 (RS) Ch 3 (always counts as 1 dc), 2 dc in ring, ch 2, *3 dc in ring, ch 2; rep from * around twice more, join rnd with a sl st in top of beg ch-3—4 ch-2 sps.

Rnd 2 Sl st in each st to first ch-2 sp, sl st in ch-2 sp, ch 3, in same ch-sp work (2 dc, ch 2, 3 dc—beg corner made), ch 1, *(3 dc, ch 2, 3 dc) in next ch-2 sp, ch 1; rep from * around twice more, join rnd with a sl st in top of beg ch-3—4 corner ch-2 sps.

Rnd 3 Sl st in each st to first corner ch-2 sp, sl st in ch-1 sp, ch 3, in same ch-sp work (2 dc, ch 2, 3 dc), ch 1, 3 dc in next ch-1 sp, ch 1, *(3 dc, ch 2, 3 dc) in next corner ch-1 sp, ch 1, 3 dc in next ch-1 sp, ch 1; rep from * around twice more, join rnd with a sl st in top of beg ch-3. Fasten off.

Rnd 4 (RS) Join MC with a sl st in any corner ch-2 sp, ch 3, in same ch-sp work (2 dc, ch 1, 3 dc), ch 1, [3 dc in next ch-1 sp, ch 1] twice, *(3 dc, ch 2, 3 dc) in next corner ch-2 sp, ch 1, [3 dc in next ch-1 sp, ch 1] twice; rep from * around twice more, join rnd with a sl st in top of beg ch-3. Fasten off, leaving a long end for sewing.

MOTIF B (MAKE 4)

Work as for motif A using B.

MOTIF C (MAKE 5)
Work as for motif A using C.

MOTIF D (MAKE 5)
Work as for motif A using D.

MOTIF E (MAKE 5)
Work as for motif A using E.

MOTIF F (MAKE 6)
Work as for motif A using F.

FINISHING
Referring to assembly diagram, arrange motifs into panels as shown. With RS tog and working through *back lps*, use MC and sl st squares tog to form panels.

Joining panels
Place panel 1 behind panel 2 with WS tog and edges even. Working through back lps of each strip, join MC with a sl st in first sts at LH edge.

Row I (RS) *Working from left to right* and through *back lps* of each panel, sc in each st across. Fasten off.

Working in the same manner, cont joining rem panels tog.

Border
With RS facing, join MC with a sc in any corner ready to work across a short edge.

Rnd I (RS) *Work 83 sc evenly spaced across short edge, 3 sc in corner, 101 sc evenly spaced across long edge, 3 sc in corner; rep from * once more omitting 3 sc in corner at end of rep, 2 sc in beg corner, join rnd with a sl st in first st—380 sts.

Rnd 2 Ch 1, sc in same sc as joining, *skip 2 sts, 5 dc in next st, skip 2 sts, sc in next st; rep from * until 5 sts before 3-sc corner, skip 2 sts, 5 dc in next st, skip 2 sts**, sc in next st, 5 dc in next st, sc in next st in 3-sc corner; rep from * 3 times more, ending last rep at **, end sc in next st, 5 dc in next st in beg corner, join rnd with a sl st in first sc. Fasten off.

Rnd 3 (RS) Join D with a sc in first dc of any corner 5-dc group, skip next st, 5 dc in next st, skip next st, sc in next st, *5 dc in next sc, [sc in center dc of next 5-dc group, 5 dc in next sc]** to next corner 5-dc group, sc in first dc of 5-dc corner, skip next st, 5 dc in next st, skip next st, sc in next st; rep from * 3 times more, ending last rep at **, join rnd with a sl st in first sc. Fasten off.

Rnd 4 (RS) Join F with a sc in center dc of any 5-dc group, 5 dc in next sc, *sc in center dc of next 5-dc group, 5 dc in next sc; rep from * around, join rnd with a sl st in first sc. Fasten off.

Rnd 5 Rep rnd 4 using C.

Rnd 6 Rep rnd 3 using A.

Rnd 7 Rep rnd 4 using E.

Rnd 8 (RS) Join MC with a sl st in any st, ch 1, *working from left to right*, sc in each st around, join rnd with a sl st in first st. Fasten off.

Assembly Diagram

Panel 1	Panel 2	Panel 3	Panel 4	Panel 5
F	E	A	D	C
E	A	D	C	F
A	D	C	F	B
D	C	F	B	E
C	F	B	E	A
F	B	E	A	D

MOTIF KEY

A Watermelon
B Mango
C Lemonade
D Limelight
E Blue mint
F Grape

All that glitters

Metallic yarn give grannies glamour plus. Amy Polcyn has used a dozen squares to create a purse that's perfect for a night out on the town.

FINISHED MEASUREMENTS

■ Approx 12½"/31.5cm wide x 8"/20cm long *(excluding handle)*

MATERIALS

■ 3 1¾oz/50g skeins (each approx 115yd/105m) of Lion Brand Yarn *Glitterspun* (acrylic/cupro/polyester) in #135 bronze (A) ⬛

■ 1 skein each in #170 gold (B) and #153 onyx (C)

■ Size F/5 (3.75mm) crochet hook *or size to obtain gauge*

■ 10"/25.5cm-wide metal purse frame with detachable rods

■ 13½"/34cm x 18"/45.5cm piece of lining fabric

■ Sewing needle and matching thread

GAUGE

One motif is 3½"/9cm square using size F/5 (3.75mm) crochet hook.

Take time to check gauge.

Note

To join yarn with a sc, make a slipknot and place on hook. Insert hook in st, yo, draw up a lp, yo and draw through both lps on hook.

MOTIF (MAKE 12)

With A, ch 4. Join ch with a sl st, forming a ring.

Rnd I (RS) Ch 3 (always counts as 1 dc), 2 dc in ring, ch 2, *3 dc in ring, ch 2; rep from * around twice more, join rnd with a sl st in top of beg ch-3—4 ch-2 sps. Fasten off.

Rnd 2 (RS) Join B with a sl st in any ch-2 sp, ch 3, in same ch-sp work (2 dc, ch 2, 3 dc—beg corner made), ch 1, *(3 dc, ch 2, 3 dc) in next ch-2 sp, ch 1; rep from * around twice more, join rnd with a sl st in top of beg ch-3—4 corner ch-1 sps. Fasten off.

Rnd 3 (RS) Join C with a sl st in any corner ch-2 sp, ch 3, in same ch-sp work (2 dc, ch 2, 3 dc), ch 1, 3 dc in next ch-1 sp, ch 1, *(3 dc, ch 2, 3 dc) in next corner ch-2 sp, ch 1, 3 dc in next ch-1 sp, ch 1; rep from * around twice more, join rnd with a sl st in top of beg ch-3. Fasten off.

Rnd 4 (RS) Join A with a sl st in any corner ch-2 sp, ch 3, in same ch-sp work (2 dc, ch 2, 3 dc), ch 1, [3 dc in next ch-1 sp, ch 1] twice, *(3 dc, ch 1, 3 dc) in next corner ch-2 sp, ch 1, [3 dc in next ch-1 sp, ch 1] twice; rep from * around twice more, join rnd with a sl st in top of beg ch-3. Fasten off, leaving long tail for sewing.

FINISHING

Back

Arrange 3 motifs wide by 2 motifs high. With WS tog and working through back lps, use yarn ends to whipstitch squares tog. Rep for front.

Sides and bottom border

Row I (RS) Join A with a sc in top LH corner ch-2 sp of back, sc in each st, ch-sp and seam to bottom LH corner ch-2 sp, (sc, ch 2, sc) in ch-sp; cont with sc in each st, each ch-sp and seam to bottom RH corner ch-2 sp, (sc, ch 2, sc) in ch-sp; cont with sc in each st, each ch-sp and seam to top RH corner ch-2 sp, sc in ch-sp. Turn.

Rows 2–5 Ch 1, sc in each st across 3 sides, working (sc, ch 2, sc) in each bottom corner ch-2 sp. Turn. When row 5 is completed, fasten off. Rep for front.

Top border

Row I (RS) Join A with a sc in top RH corner ch-2 sp of back, sc in each st, each ch-sp and seam to top LH corner ch-2 sp, sc in ch-sp. Turn.

Rows 2–8 Ch 1, sc in each st across. Turn. When row 8 is completed, fasten off. Rep for front. With WS of back and front facing, whipstitch tog along sides and bottom borders. Fold each top border in half to WS and hem, forming casings for purse frame rods.

Lining

With RS facing, fold lining fabric in half lengthwise so it measures 13½"/34cm x 9"/23cm. Sew side seams using a ½"/1.3cm seam allowance. Fold top edge 1"/2.5cm to WS; press. Insert lining into purse. Pin lining in place so top edge butts bottom edge of casings and is ¼"/.5cm from remaining top edges of purse. Slip-stitch top edge of lining in place. Remove rods from purse frame and insert through casings. Attach rods to frame.

Short and sweet

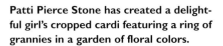

Patti Pierce Stone has created a delightful girl's cropped cardi featuring a ring of grannies in a garden of floral colors.

SIZES

Instructions are written for girl's size 4/6. Changes for 8/10 are in parentheses.

FINISHED MEASUREMENTS

■ Chest 23 (26)"/58.5 (66)cm
■ Length 11½ (13¼)"/29 (33.5)cm

MATERIALS

■ 2 (3) 1¾oz/50g skeins (each approx 93yd/85m) of Rowan/Westminster Fibers, Inc. *Handknit Cotton* (cotton) in #313 slick (D) ▣
■ 1 skein each in #309 celery (A), #251 ecru (B) and #303 sugar (C)
■ Sizes E/4 and G/6 (3.5 and 4mm) crochet hook *or sizes to obtain gauge*

GAUGE

Motif measures 3¼"/8cm square using larger crochet hook.
Take time to check gauge.

STITCH GLOSSARY

dc2tog [Yo, insert hook into next st (or row), yo and draw up a lp, yo and draw through 2 lps on hook] twice, yo and draw through all 3 lps on hook.

WHOLE MOTIF [MAKE 10 (12)]

With larger hook and A, ch 3. Join ch with a sl st, forming a ring.

Rnd 1 (RS) Ch 1, 8 sc in ring, join rnd with a sl st in first sc. Fasten off.

Rnd 2 (RS) Join B with a sl st in same st as joining, ch 5 (counts as 1 dc and ch 2), *dc in next st, ch 2; rep from * around, join rnd with a sl st in 3rd ch of beg ch-5—8 dc and ch-2 sps. Fasten off.

Rnd 3 (RS) Join C with a sl st in any ch-2 sp, (sc, hdc, dc) in same ch-sp, dc in next dc, (dc, hdc, sc) in next ch-2 sp, ch 5, [(sc, hdc, dc) in next ch-2 sp, dc in next dc, (dc, hdc, sc) in next ch-2 sp, ch 5] 3 times, join rnd with a sl st in first sc—4 petals and ch-5 lps. Fasten off.

Rnd 4 (RS) Join A with a sl st in any ch-5 lp, ch 2 (counts as 1 hdc), (hdc, ch 2, 2 hdc) in same lp—beg corner made, ch 3, sc in center dc of next petal, ch 3, [(2 hdc, ch 2, 2 hdc) in next ch-5 lp, ch 3, sc in center dc of next petal, ch 3] 3 times, join rnd with a sl st in top of beg ch-2.

Rnd 5 Ch 1, working in *back lps* (except corner ch-2 sps), sc in same place as joining, sc in next hdc, 3 sc in corner ch-2 sp, [sc in each st and ch to next corner ch-2 sp, 3 sc in corner ch-sp] 3 times, sc in each st and ch to end, join rnd with a sl st in first sc. Fasten off.

TRIANGLE MOTIF (MAKE 2)

With larger hook and A, ch 3. Join ch with a sl st, forming a ring.

Rnd I (RS) Ch 1, 6 sc in ring, join rnd with a sl st in first sc. Fasten off. You will now be working in rows.

Row 2 (RS) Join B with a sl st in any sc, ch 5 (counts as 1 dc and ch 2), [dc in next st, ch 2] 3 times, dc in next st—5 dc and 4 ch-2 sps. Fasten off.

Row 3 (RS) Join C with a sl st in 3rd ch of beg ch-5 of row below, ch 3 (counts as 1 dc), (dc, hdc, sc) in first ch-2 sp, ch 5, (sc, hdc, dc) in next ch-2 sp, dc in next dc, (dc, hdc, sc) in next ch-2 sp, ch 5, (sc, hdc, dc) in last ch-2 sp, dc in last st—one whole petal, 2 half-petals and 2 ch-5 lps. Fasten off.

Row 4 (RS) Join A with a sl st in top of beg ch-3 of row below, ch 3 (counts as 1 hdc and ch 1), 2 hdc in same place as joining, ch 3, sc in first ch-5 lp, ch 3, (2 hdc, ch 2, 2 hdc) in next ch-5 lp, ch 3, sc in next ch-5 lp, ch 3, (2 hdc, ch 1, hdc) in last st. Fasten off. You will now be working in the round.

Rnd 5 (RS) Join A with a sl st in back lp in 2nd unworked sc of rnd 1, ch 1, sc in same st, working through *back lps* of sts and ch, cont to sc in next st, 2 sc in side edge of each of next 3 rows, 3 sc in corner ch-1 sp, sc in each st and ch to center ch-2 sp, 5 sc in ch-2 sp, sc in each st and ch to next corner ch-1 sp, 3 sc in corner ch-1 sp, 2 sc in side edge of each of next 3 rows, sc in rem sc of rnd 1, join rnd with a sl st in first sc. Fasten off.

JOINING MOTIFS

Place 2 motifs WS tog. With smaller hook, join B with a sl st in 2nd corner sc of front motif, ch 2, sl st in 2nd corner sc of back motif, [ch 2, skip next 2 sts of front motif, sl st in next st, ch 2, skip next 2 sts of back motif, sl st in next st] 4 times, ch 2, sl st in 2nd corner sc of front motif, ch 2, sl st in 2nd corner sc of motif at back. Fasten off. Referring to assembly diagram for size being made and for joining whole and triangle motifs tog to form border.

BACK

With RS of border facing and larger hook, skip RH triangle motif, then first 6 sc of next whole motif. *Working in back lps only*, join D with a sl st in back lp of next sc, ch 2, hdc in same st as joining, then 50 (62) sts more evenly spaced along edge, working hdc in each st and dc in joining chs to within last 6 sc of last whole motif—51 (63) sts. Turn.

Row I (WS) Ch 1, sc in first st, *ch 2, skip next st, sc in next st; rep from * to end. Turn.

Row 2 Ch 3, *hdc in ch-2 sp, dc in next st; rep from * to end. Turn.

Rep last 2 rows 4 (6) times more. Fasten off, leaving a long end for sewing.

Working through *back lps*, whipstitch top edge of back to corresponding motifs on opposite edge of border.

Edging

With RS facing and larger hook, join D with a sl st in center top back edge.

Rnd 1 Ch 3 (counts as 1 dc), working in *back lps*, dc in each st around, join rnd with a sl st in top of beg ch-3.

Rnd 2 Ch 1, working in *back lps and from left to right*, sc in each st around, join rnd with a sl st in beg ch-1. Fasten off.

Armhole bands

With RS facing and larger hook, join D with a sl st in center bottom armhole edge.

Rnd 1 Ch 3 (counts as 1 dc), working in *back lps* of sts (and side edges of rows), dc evenly around, with dc2tog in each bottom corner and center of shoulder, join rnd with a sl st in top of beg ch-3.

Rnd 2 Ch 1, sc in each st around, join rnd with a sl st in first sc.

Rnd 3 Ch 3, dc in each st around, join rnd with a sl st in top of beg ch-3.

Rnd 4 Ch 1, working in *back lps and from left to right*, sc in each st around, join rnd with a sl st in beg ch-1. Fasten off.

Motif Border Assembly Diagram (Size 4/6)

19½"

Motif Border Assembly Diagram (Size 8/10)

22¾"

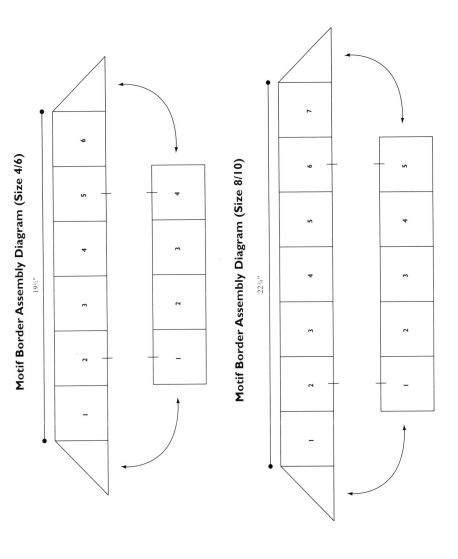

Variegated squares add bold color flair to the hem of this captivating capelet. The body is worked in a cluster and chain stitch pattern that partners perfectly with the cluster-stitch grannies. Designed by Linda Cyr.

SIZES
Instructions are written for one size.

FINISHED MEASUREMENTS
■ Lower edge 56"/142cm
■ Length 17"/43cm

MATERIALS
■ 2 4oz/113g hanks (each approx 225yd/ 206m) of Lorna's Laces *Shepherd Worsted* (superwash wool) in #16ns charcoal (MC)

(4)

■ 1 hank each in #56 mountain creek (A) and #23ns berry (B)
■ Size I/9 (5.5mm) crochet hook *or size to obtain gauge*

GAUGES
■ One motif to 4½"/11.5cm square using size I/9 (5.5mm) crochet hook.
■ 13 sts and 8 rws to 4"/10cm in dc pat using size I/9 (5.5mm) crochet hook.
Take time to check gauges.

STITCH GLOSSARY
CL (cluster st) In same sp work [yo, insert hook into st, yo and draw up a lp, yo and draw through 2 lps on hook] 3 times, yo and draw through all 4 lps on hook.

MOTIF (MAKE 12)
With A, ch 6. Join ch with a sl st, forming a ring.

Rnd 1 (RS) Ch 3 (counts as 1 dc), [yo, insert hook into st, yo and draw up a lp, yo and draw through 2 lps on hook] twice, yo and draw through all 3 lps on hook (beg CL made), ch 3, [CL in ring, ch 3] 7 times, join rnd with a sl st in top of beg ch-3—8 CL.

Rnd 2 Sl st in first ch-3 sp, ch 3 (counts as 1 dc), in same ch-sp work (2 dc, ch 3, 3 dc—beg corner made), ch 3, 3 dc in next ch-3 sp, *(3 dc, ch 3, 3 dc) in next ch-3 sp, ch 3, 3 dc in next ch-3 sp, ch 3; rep from * around twice more, join rnd with a sl st in top of beg ch-3—4 corner ch-3 sps.

Rnd 3 Ch 1, sc in same sp as joining, sc in next 2 sts, *(2 sc, ch 2, 2 sc) in next corner ch-3 sp, sc in next 9 sts; rep from * around twice more, end (2 sc, ch 2, 2 sc) in last ch-3 sp, sc in last 6 sts, join rnd with a sl st in first st.

Rnd 4 Ch 1, sc in same sp as joining, sc in next 4 sts, *2 sc in next corner ch-2 sp, sc in next 13 sts; rep from * around twice more, end 2 sc in last ch-2 sp, sc in last 8 sts, join rnd with a sl st in first st. Fasten off.

Rnd 5 (RS) Join MC with a sc in first of 2 corner sts, sc in same st as joining, 2 sc in next sc, sc in next 13 sts, *2 sc in next 2 corner sts, sc in next 13 sts; rep from * around twice more, join rnd with a sl st in first st. Fasten off, leaving a long end for sewing.

Joining

With RS tog and using MC, sl st motifs tog, forming a strip. There are 17 sts across top edge of each square.

Edging

With RS facing, join MC with a sl st in first of 2 corner sts of top LH corner.

Next rnd (RS) Ch 5 (counts as 1 dc and ch 2), 3 dc in 2nd corner st, skip next 3 sts, [3 dc in next st, skip next 2 sts] 4 times, 3 dc in first of next 2 corner sts, ch 2, 3 dc into 2nd corner st, skip next 3 sts, [3 dc in next st, skip next 2 sts] 3 times, 3 dc in next st, *3 dc into first st of next square, skip next 3 sts, [3 dc in next st, skip next 2 sts] 3 times, 3 dc in next st; rep from * across bottom edge, 3 dc in 1st st of 2 corner sts, ch 2, 3 dc in 2nd of 2 corner sts, [skip next 2 sts, 3 dc in next st] 4 times, skip next 3 sts, 3 dc in 1st of 2 corner sts, ch 2, then rep from * beg in 2nd of 2 corner sts along opp edge, end 2 dc in same st as joining, join rnd with a sl st in 3rd ch of beg ch-5. Turn.

Working across top edge of strip only, cont as foll:

Body

Row 1 (WS) *Ch 5, sc between next 2 3-dc groups; rep from *, end ch 5, sc in ch-2 sp of row below. Turn.

Row 2 (RS) Ch 5, 3 dc in each ch-5 sp across, end dtr in ch-5 t-ch of row below. Turn.

Row 3 *Ch 5, sc between next 2 3-dc groups; rep from *, end ch 5, sc in ch-5 t-ch of row below. Turn. Change to B.

Rows 4 and 5 With B, rep rows 2 and 3. Cont with MC only as foll:

Row 6 Ch 5, 3 dc in next 5 ch-5 sps, *2 dc in next 2 ch-5 sps, 3 dc in next 4 ch-5 sps; rep from *, end 3 dc in last 2 ch-5 sps, dtr in ch-5 t-ch of row below. Turn.

Row 7 Ch 5, sc between next 2 dc-groups, *[ch 5, sc between next 2 dc-groups] 5 times, skip sp between 2-dc groups; rep from *, end [ch 5, sc between next 2 dc-groups] 5 times, ch 5, sc in ch-5 t-ch of row below. Turn.

Rows 8 and 9 Rep rows 2 and 3.

Row 10 Ch 5, 3 dc in first 2 ch-5 sps, *2 dc in next 2 ch-5 sps, 3 dc in next 3 ch-5 sps; rep from *, end dtr in ch-5 t-ch of row below. Turn.

Row 11 [Ch 5, sc between next 2 dc-groups] 3 times, skip sp between 2-dc groups, *[ch 5, sc between next 2 dc-groups] 4 times, skip sp between 2-dc groups; rep from *, end [ch 5, sc between next 2 dc-groups] twice, sc in ch-5 t-ch of row below. Turn.

Rows 12 and 13 Rep rows 2 and 3.

Row 14 Ch 5, 3 dc in first 2 ch-5 sps, *2 dc in next 2 ch-5 sps, 3 dc in next 2 ch-5 sps; rep from *, end dtr in ch-5 t-ch of row below. Turn.

Row 15 [Ch 5, sc between next 2 dc-groups] twice, skip sp between 2-dc groups, *[ch 5, sc between next 2 dc-groups] 3 times, skip sp between 2-dc groups; rep from *, end [ch 5, sc between next 2 dc-groups] twice, sc in ch-5 t-ch of row below. Turn.

Rows 16 and 17 Rep rows 2 and 3.

Row 18 Ch 5, 3 dc in first 2 ch-5 sps, *2 dc in next 2 ch-5 sps, 3 dc in next ch-5 sp; rep from *, end dtr in ch-5 t-ch of row below. Turn.

Row 19 Ch 5, sc between first 2 dc-groups, *skip sp between 2-dc groups, [ch 5, sc between next 2 dc-groups] twice; rep from *, end, sc in ch-5 t-ch of row below. Turn.

Row 20 Rep row 2. Turn.

Edging

Next rnd (WS) Sl st in each st across neck edge, ch 1, sc evenly along side edge to corner ch-sp, 3 sc in corner ch-sp, sc in each st across bottom edge to corner ch-sp, 3 sc in corner ch-sp, sc evenly along side edge to end, join rnd with a sl st in first sl st. Fasten off.

FINISHING

Ties

For each tie, cut six 34"/86.5cm strands of B. Thread strands through ch-sp at top RH edge. Even up strand ends. Divide strands into 3 equal bundles. Braid to within last 1"/2.5cm. Tie ends in an overhand knot; trim ends even. Rep for top LH edge.

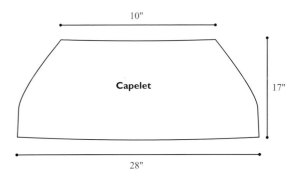

10"

Capelet

17"

28"

Pillow power

Create patchwork perfection with hexagon-shaped grannies. Linda Permann has designed two pillows in a pretty palette of country colors to show off their graphic versatility.

FINISHED MEASUREMENTS

■ Approx 12"/30.5cm long x 16"/40.5cm wide

MATERIALS

■ 1 3½oz/100g hank (approx 225yd/206m) of Louet North America *Gems Sport* (superwash merino wool) each in #5 goldilocks, #35 mustard, #2 ginger, #62 citrus orange, #11 cherry red, #58 burgundy and #26 crabapple (**2**)

■ Size F/5 (3.5 mm) crochet hook *or size to obtain gauge*

■ Two 12"/30.5cm x 16"/40.5cm pillow forms

GAUGE

Six-point motif is 4⅛"/10.5cm (at widest point) using size F/5 (3.5mm) crochet hook. *Take time to check gauge.*

Note

To join yarn with a sc, make a slipknot and place on hook. Insert hook in st, yo, draw up a lp, yo and draw through both lps on hook.

COLOR SEQUENCES

Goldilocks motifs
A crabapple, **B** citrus orange, **C** mustard, **D** goldilocks

Mustard motifs
A cherry red, **B** crabapple, **C** ginger, **D** mustard

Ginger motifs
A citrus orange, **B** cherry red, **C** goldilocks, **D** ginger

Citrus orange motifs
A goldilocks, **B** ginger, **C** burgundy, **D** citrus orange

Cherry red motifs
A crabapple, **B** burgundy, **C** citrus orange, **D** cherry red

Burgundy motifs
A ginger, **B** citrus orange, **C** crabapple, **D** burgundy

Crabapple motifs
A mustard, **B** goldilocks, **C** cherry red, **D** crabapple

SIX-POINT MOTIF

To make an adjustable ring, use A to make a slipknot 10"/25.5cm from free end of yarn. Place slipknot on hook, then wrap free end of yarn twice around your first and second fingers on your left hand. Now work from yarn coming from ball as follows:

Rnd I (RS) Ch 3 (counts as 1 dc), 11 dc in ring, pull free end of yarn to close circle, then join rnd with a sl st in 3rd ch of beg ch-3—12 dc. Fasten off.

Rnd 2 (RS) Join B with a sl st in sp between any 2 dc of rnd below, ch 3 (counts as 1 dc), dc in same sp, cont to work 2 dc in sp between each dc around, join rnd with a sl st in top of beg ch-3—24 dc. Fasten off.

Rnd 3 (RS) Join C with a sl st in sp between any 2-dc groups of rnd below, ch 3 (counts as 1 dc), 2 dc in same sp, cont to work 3 dc in sp between each 2-dc group around, join rnd with a sl st in top of beg ch-3—36 dc. Fasten off.

Rnd 4 (RS) Join D with a sc in sp between any 3-dc groups of rnd below, ch 3, *sc in sp between next 2 3-dc groups, ch 3; rep from * around, join rnd with a sl st in first sc—12 sc and 12 ch-3 sps. Do *not* fasten off.

Rnd 5 Sl st in first ch-3 sp, ch 3 (counts as first dc), 3 dc in same ch-sp, (4 dc, ch 2, 4 dc) in next ch-3 sp, *4 dc in next ch-3 sp, (4 dc, ch 2, 4 dc) in next ch-3 sp; rep from * around, join rnd with a sl st in top of beg ch-3. Fasten off, leaving a long tail for sewing.

TWO-POINT MOTIF

With A, ch 4.

Row 1 (RS) Skip first 3 ch (counts as 1 dc), 6 dc in last ch—7 dc. Fasten off. *Do not turn.*

Row 2 (RS) Join B with a sl st in top of ch-3 of row below, ch 3 (counts as 1 dc), dc between first and 2nd dc of row below, [2 dc between next 2 dc] 4 times, dc between next dc and last dc, dc in last dc—12 dc. Fasten off. *Do not turn.*

Row 3 (RS) Join C with a sl st in top of ch-3 of row below, ch 3 (counts as 1 dc), dc between first and 2nd dc of row below, 3 dc between first 2-dc and 2nd 2-dc group, [3 dc between next 2 2-dc groups] 4 times, dc between last 2 dc, dc in last dc—19 dc. Fasten off. Turn.

Row 4 (WS) Join D with a sc in first dc, ch 1, sc in sp between first 2-dc and next 3-dc group, [ch 3, sc in sp between next 2 3-dc group] 5 times, ch 1, sc in top of ch-3 t-ch of row below—5 ch-3 sps and 2 ch-1 sps. Turn.

Row 5 (RS) Ch 3 (counts as first dc), dc in ch-1 sp, *4 dc in next ch-3 sp, (4 dc, ch 2, 4 dc) in next ch-3 sp; rep from * once more, 4 dc in last ch-3 sp, dc in ch-1 sp, dc in last sc. Fasten off, leaving long tail for sewing.

THREE-POINT MOTIF

Work as for two-point motif through row 4—5 ch-3 sps and 2 ch-1 sps. Turn.

Row 5 (RS) Ch 3 (counts as first dc), dc in ch-1 sp, *(4 dc, ch 2, 4 dc) in next ch-3 sp, 4 dc in next ch-3 sp; rep from * once more, (4 dc , ch 2, 4 dc) in last ch-3 sp, dc in ch-1 sp, dc in last sc. Fasten off, leaving long tail for sewing.

RANDOM MOTIFS PILLOW

Front

Make motifs in color sequences as foll:

Goldilocks 1 six-point motif, 1 two-point motif.

Mustard 1 six-point motif, 2 three-point motifs.

Ginger 2 six-point motifs, 1 two-point motif.

Citrus orange 1 six-point motif, 2 three-point motifs.

Cherry red 2 six-point motifs, 1 three-point motif and 1 two-point motif.

Burgundy 2 six-point motifs, 1 three-point motif.

Crabapple 1 six-point motif, 2 three-point motifs and 1 two-point motif.

Back

With ginger, ch 56.

Row 1 (RS) Dc in 4th ch from hook and in each ch across—53 dc. Turn.

Rows 2–14 Ch 3, dc in each st across. Turn. When row 13 is completed, fasten off, turn.

Row 15 (WS) Join goldilocks with a sl st in first dc, ch 3, dc in same st, dc in each dc across. Turn.

Rows 16–26 Ch 3, dc in each st across. Turn. When row 25 is completed, fasten off, turn.

Row 27 (WS) Join ginger with a sl st in first dc, ch 3, dc in same st, dc in each dc across. Turn.

Rows 28–39 Ch 3, dc in each st across. Turn. When row 39 is completed, fasten off, leaving long tail for sewing.

Front

Make motifs in color sequences as foll:

Goldilocks 2 six-point motifs, 4 three-point motifs.

Citrus orange 2 six-point motifs, 4 three-point motifs.

Burgundy 2 six-point motifs, 4 two-point motifs.

Crabapple 4 six-point motifs.

Back

Work as for random motifs pillow using crabapple, burgundy and cherry red.

FINISHING

Refer to assembly diagram. With WS tog and working through back lps, use yarn ends to whipstitch motifs tog to form pillow front. Place pillow front and back RS tog. Using colors to match back colors, whipstitch along three sides, leaving one short side open. Turn right side out. Insert pillow form; whipstitch opening closed.

Assembly Diagram—Random Motifs Pillow

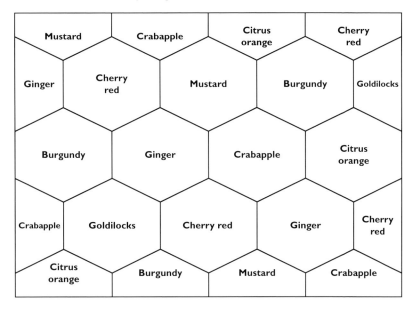

Assembly Diagram—Diamond Motifs Pillow

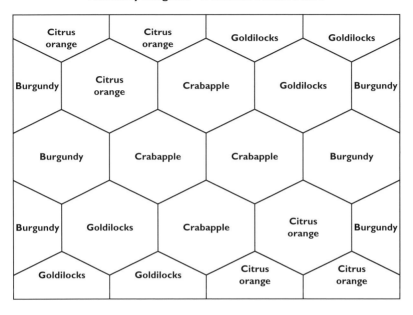

Citrus orange	Citrus orange	Goldilocks	Goldilocks
Burgundy	Citrus orange	Crabapple	Goldilocks	Burgundy
Burgundy	Crabapple	Crabapple	Burgundy
Burgundy	Goldilocks	Crabapple	Citrus orange	Burgundy
Goldilocks	Goldilocks	Citrus orange	Citrus orange

Designer Marty Miller has fashioned three basic granny squares into a fabulous shoulder-hugging shrug. Self-striping yarn creates an endless palette of bright crayon colors.

SIZES

Instructions are written for Small/Medium. Changes for Large/X-Large are in parentheses.

FINISHED MEASUREMENTS

Length 18 (20)"/45.5 (51)cm
Upper arm 15 (17)"/38 (43)cm

MATERIALS

▪ 8 (9) 1¾oz/50g skeins (each approx 110yd/100m) of Noro/KFI *Kureyon* (4) (wool) in #182 multi

▪ Size J/10 (6mm) crochet hook *or size to obtain gauge*

GAUGE

Motif measures 15 (17)"/38 (43)cm square using size J/10 (6mm) crochet hook.
Take time to check gauge.

STITCH GLOSSARY

FPdc (front post dc) Yo, working from front to back to front, insert hook around post of stitch in rnd below, yo and draw up a lp, [yo and draw through 2 lps on hook] twice.

BPdc (back post dc) Yo, working from back to front to back, insert hook around post of stitch in rnd below, yo and draw up a lp, [yo and draw through 2 lps on hook] twice.

MOTIF I

Ch 4. Join ch with a sl st, forming a ring.

Rnd I (RS) Ch 3 (always counts as 1 dc), 2 dc in ring, ch 1, *3 dc in ring, ch 1; rep from * around twice more, join rnd with a sl st in top of beg ch-3—4 ch-1 sps.

Rnd 2 Sl st in each st to first ch-1 sp, sl st in ch-1 sp, ch 3, in same ch-sp work (2 dc, ch 1, 3 dc—beg corner made), ch 1, *(3 dc, ch 1, 3 dc) in next ch-1 sp, ch 1; rep from * around twice more, join rnd with a sl st in top of beg ch-3—4 corner ch-1 sps.

Rnd 3 Sl st in each st to first corner ch-1 sp, sl st in ch-1 sp, ch 3, in same ch-sp work (2 dc, ch 1, 3 dc), ch 1, 3 dc in next ch-1 sp, ch 1, *(3 dc, ch 1, 3 dc) in next corner ch-1 sp, ch 1, 3 dc in next ch-1 sp, ch 1; rep from * around twice more, join rnd with a sl st in top of beg ch-3.

Rnd 4 Sl st in each st to first corner ch-1 sp, sl st in ch-1 sp, ch 3, in same ch-sp work (2 dc, ch 1, 3 dc), ch 1, [3 dc in next ch-1 sp, ch 1] twice, *(3 dc, ch 1, 3 dc) in next corner ch-1 sp, ch 1, [3 dc in next ch-1 sp, ch 1] twice; rep from * around twice more, join rnd with a sl st in top of beg ch-3.

Rnd 5 Sl st in each st to first corner ch-1 sp, sl st in ch-1 sp, ch 3, in same ch-sp work (2 dc, ch 1, 3 dc), ch 1, [3 dc in next ch-1 sp, ch 1] 3 times, *(3 dc, ch 1, 3 dc) in next corner ch-1 sp, ch 1, [3 dc in next ch-1 sp, ch 1] 3

times; rep from * around twice more, join rnd with a sl st in top of beg ch-3.

Rnd 6 Sl st in each st to first corner ch-1 sp, sl st in ch-1 sp, ch 3, in same ch-sp work (2 dc, ch 1, 3 dc), ch 1, [3 dc in next ch-1 sp, ch 1] 4 times, *(3 dc, ch 1, 3 dc) in next corner ch-1 sp, ch 1, [3 dc in next ch-1 sp, ch 1] 4 times; rep from * around twice more, join rnd with a sl st in top of beg ch-3.

Rnds 7–11 (7–12) Rep rnd 6, working one more 3-dc group between corners every rnd. When rnd 11 (12) is completed, fasten off.

MOTIF 2

Rep rnds 1–10 (1–11) of motif 1.

Note: You will be joining the motifs along one edge in the ch-1 sps. Instead of ch 1 between the 3-dc groups, you will be working a sc in the corresponding ch-1 sp of the motif 1.

Rnd 11 (12) (Joining) Sl st in each st to first corner ch-1 sp, ch 3, 2 dc in same ch-1 sp, place motif 1 behind motif 2, WS tog and matching corners, sc in corresponding ch-1 sp on motif 1, 3 dc in same corner ch-2 sp of motif 2, *sc in next ch-1 sp of motif 1, 3 dc in next ch-1 sp of motif 2*; rep from * to * to next corner, sc in next ch-1 sp of motif 1, 3 dc in corner ch-1 sp on motif 2, sc in corner ch-1 sp of motif 1, 3 dc in same corner ch-1 sp of motif 2, ch 1, **(3 dc, ch-1) in each ch-1 sp of motif 2 to next corner, (3 dc, ch 1, 3 dc) in corner ch-1 sp, ch 1; rep from ** around, join rnd with a sl st in top of beg ch-3. Fasten off.

MOTIF 3

Rep rnds 1–11 (1–12) of motif 2, joining motif 3 to motif 1 in last rnd.

FINISHING

With WS tog, fold strip of motifs in half lengthwise. Working through both thicknesses, join yarn with a sl st at one end.

Sleeve joining

Row 1 Ch 1, *sc in 2nd st of 3-dc group on front edge, ch 1, sc in 2nd dc of 3-dc group on back edge, ch 1, sc in ch-1 sp on front edge, ch 1, sc in ch-1 sp on back edge; rep from * until 8 3-dc groups have been joined. Fasten off.

Rep at opposite end.

Edging

Join yarn with a sl st in underarm seam.

Rnd 1 (RS) Ch 1, sc in each dc and ch-1 sp around, join rnd with a sl st in first sc.

Rnd 2 Ch 3 (counts as 1 dc), skip first sc, dc in each rem sc around, join rnd with a sl st in top of beg ch-3—136 (140) dc.

Rnd 3 Ch 2 (counts as 1 BPdc), FPdc around next dc, *BPdc around next dc, FPdc around next dc; rep from * around, join rnd with a sl st in top of beg ch-2.

Rnds 4 and 5 Ch 2 (counts as 1 BPdc), FPdc around next FPdc, *BPdc around next BPdc, FPdc around next FPdc; rep from * around, join rnd with a sl st in top of beg ch-2. When rnd 5 is completed, fasten off.

Cuffs

Join yarn with a sl st in sleeve seam.

Rnd I (RS) Ch 1, work 34 (38) sc evenly spaced around sleeve edge, join rnd with a sl st in first sc.

Rnds 2 and 3 Rep rnds 2 and 3 of edging.

Rnds 4–11 Rep rnd 4 of edging. When rnd 11 is completed, fasten off.

Weave in ends.

TOTE BAG

Orange crush

You don't have to wear green to be green. Here, two extra-large squares become one terrific eco-friendly tote for carrying everything from groceries to your latest crochet project. Designed by Marty Miller.

SIZE
Instructions are written for one size.

FINISHED MEASUREMENTS
■ Approx 12½"/31.5cm wide x 14"/ 35.5cm long *(excluding handles)*

MATERIALS
■ 4 1¾oz/50g skeins (each approx 120yd/ 111m) of Berroco, Inc. *Suede* (nylon ribbon) in #3739 campfire (**4**)
■ Size H/8 (5mm) crochet hook *or size to obtain gauges*

GAUGES
■ One motif to 12"/30.5cm square using size H/8 (5mm) crochet hook.
■ 16 sts and 18¼ rows to 4"/10cm over sc using size H/8 (5mm) crochet hook.
Take time to check gauges.

BACK
Ch 4. Join ch with a sl st forming a ring.

Rnd I (RS) Ch 3 (always counts as 1 dc), 2 dc in ring, ch 1, *3 dc in ring, ch 1; rep from * around twice more, join rnd with a sl st in top of beg ch-3—4 ch-1 sps.

Rnd 2 Sl st in each st to first ch-1 sp, sl st in ch-1 sp, ch 3, in same ch-sp work (2 dc, ch 1, 3 dc—beg corner made), ch 1, *(3 dc, ch 1, 3 dc) in next ch-1 sp, ch 1; rep from * around twice more, join rnd with a sl st in top of beg ch-3—4 corner ch-1 sps.

Rnd 3 Sl st in each st to first corner ch-1 sp, sl st in ch-1 sp, ch 3, in same ch-sp work (2 dc, ch 1, 3 dc), ch 1, 3 dc in next ch-1 sp, ch 1, * (3 dc, ch 1, 3 dc) in next corner ch-1 sp, ch 1, 3 dc in next ch-1 sp, ch 1; rep from * around twice more, join rnd with a sl st in top of beg ch-3.

Rnd 4 Sl st in each st to first corner ch-1 sp, sl st in ch-1 sp, ch 3, in same ch-sp work (2 dc, ch 1, 3 dc), ch 1, [3 dc in next ch-1 sp, ch 1] twice, *(3 dc, ch 1, 3 dc) in next corner ch-1 sp, ch 1, [3 dc in next ch-1 sp, ch 1] twice; rep from * around twice more, join rnd with a sl st in top of beg ch-3.

Rnd 5 Sl st in each st to first corner ch-1 sp, sl st in ch-1 sp, ch 3, in same ch-sp work (2 dc, ch 1, 3 dc), ch 1, [3 dc in next ch-1 sp, ch 1] 3 times, *(3 dc, ch 1, 3 dc) in next corner ch-1 sp, ch 1, [3 dc in next ch-1 sp, ch 1] 3 times; rep from * around twice more, join rnd with a sl st in top of beg ch-3.

Rnd 6 Sl st in each st to first corner ch-1 sp, sl st in ch-1 sp, ch 3, in same ch-sp work (2 dc, ch 1, 3 dc), ch 1, [3 dc in next ch-1 sp, ch 1] 4 times, *(3 dc, ch 1, 3 dc) in next corner ch-1 sp, ch 1, [3 dc in next ch-1 sp, ch 1] 4 times; rep from * around twice more, join rnd with a sl st in top of beg ch-3.

Rnds 7–11 Rep rnd 6, working one more 3-dc group between corners every rnd. When rnd 11 is completed, fasten off.

FRONT

Work as for back through rnd 11. Do not fasten off, sl st in each st to first corner ch-1 sp.

FINISHING

Joining side edges

Place front and back tog, WS facing and edges even.

Ch 1, *working through both thicknesses*, sc in corner ch-1 sp, *sc in each dc and ch-1 sp to next corner, 3 sc in corner ch-1 sp; rep from * twice more, omitting 3 sc in corner ch-1 sp in last rep, end sc in next corner ch-1 sp. Do *not* fasten off.

Top edging

Rnd 1 (RS) Ch 1, sc in same ch-1 sp as last sc, sc in each dc and ch-1 sp to next corner ch-1 sp, sc in corner ch-1 sp; skip side seam, sc in corner ch-1 sp of opposite side, sc in each dc and ch-1 sp to last corner ch-1 sp, sc in corner ch-1 sp, skip side seam, join rnd with a sl st in first st—90 sts.

Rnds 2–4 Ch 1, sc in each sc around, join rnd with a sl st in first st.

Handles

Rnd 5 Ch 1, sc in first 10 sts, ch 60, skip next 25 sts, sc in next 20 sts, ch 60, skip next 25 sts, sc in last 10 sts, join rnd with a sl st in first sc.

Rnd 6 Ch 1, sc in each sc and ch around, join rnd with a sl st in first sc—160 sts.

Rnd 7 Ch 1, sc in each sc around, join rnd with a sl st in first sc.

Rnd 8 Rep rnd 7. Fasten off.

Weave in ends.

SUN HAT

Hats off to grannies!

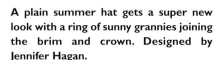

A plain summer hat gets a super new look with a ring of sunny grannies joining the brim and crown. Designed by Jennifer Hagan.

SIZES

Instructions are written for one size.

FINISHED MEASUREMENTS

- Head circumference 21"/53.5cm
- Depth 7½"/19cm *(excluding brim)*

MATERIALS

- 1 3½oz/100g hank (approx 140yd/128m) of Plymouth Yarn Co., *Fantasy Natural* (mercerized cotton) each in #7360 flax (MC), #1242 lemon (A), #1404 sunflower (B) and #8011 lime (C) ▨
- Size H/8 (5mm) crochet hook *or size to obtain gauges*
- Small safety pin
- Tapestry needle

GAUGES

- One motif is 3"/7.5cm square using size H/8 (5mm) crochet hook.
- 16 sts and 20 rnds to 4"/10cm over sc using size H/8 (5mm) crochet hook.
Take time to check gauges.

Note

To join yarn with a sc, make a slipknot and place on hook. Insert hook in lp in st, yo, draw up a lp, yo and draw through both lps on hook.

HATBAND

Motif (make 7)

With A, ch 6. Join ch with a sl st, forming a ring.

Rnd 1 (RS) Ch 3 (always counts as 1 dc), 2 dc in ring, ch 2, *3 dc in ring, ch 2; rep from * around twice more, join rnd with a sl st in top of beg ch-3—4 ch-2 sps. Fasten off.

Rnd 2 (RS) Join B with a sl st in any ch-2 sp, ch 3, in same ch-sp work (2 dc, ch 2, 3 dc—beg corner made), ch 1, *(3 dc, ch 2, 3 dc) in next ch-1 sp, ch 1; rep from * around twice more, join rnd with a sl st in top of beg ch-3—4 corner ch-2 sps. Fasten off.

Rnd 3 (RS) Join C with a sc in dc before any corner ch-2 sp, 3 sc in corner ch-2 sp, cont with sc in each dc around, working 3 sc in each corner ch-2 sp, join rnd with a sl st in first sc. Fasten off, leaving long tail for sewing.

With WS tog and working through *back lps*, whipstitch squares tog in a strip, then whipstitch strip tog, forming a ring.

Top edging

With RS facing, join C with a sc in top right corner sc of any motif, sc in each of next 75 sc, join rnd with a sl st in first sc—75 sts. Fasten off.

Bottom edging

With RS facing, join C with a sc in top right

corner sc of any motif on opposite edge, then cont to sc in each of next 75 sc, join rnd with a sl st in first sc—76 sts. Fasten off.

CROWN

Rnd 1 (RS) With RS facing, join MC with a sc in any sc of top edge, then cont to sc in each st around, inc 2 sts evenly spaced—78 sts. *Do not join.* Mark last st made with the safety pin. You will be working in a spiral, marking the last st made with the safety pin to indicate end of rnd.

Rnds 2 and 3 Sc in each st around.

Rnd 4 *Sc in next 11 sts, sc2tog; rep from * around—72 sts.

Rnds 5 and 6 Sc in each st around.

Rnd 7 *Sc in next 10 sts, sc2tog; rep from * around—66 sts.

Rnd 8 Sc in each st around.

Rnd 9 *Sc in next 9 sts, sc2tog; rep from * around—60 sts.

Rnd 10 Sc in each st around.

Rnd 11 *Sc in next 8 sts, sc2tog; rep from * around—54 sts.

Rnd 12 *Sc in next 7 sts, sc2tog; rep from * around—48 sts.

Rnd 13 *Sc in next 6 sts, sc2tog; rep from * around—42 sts.

Rnd 14 *Sc in next 5 sts, sc2tog; rep from * around—36 sts.

Rnd 15 *Sc in next 4 sts, sc2tog; rep from * around—30 sts.

Rnd 16 *Sc in next 3 sts, sc2tog; rep from * around—24 sts.

Rnd 17 *Sc in next 2 sts, sc2tog; rep from * around—18 sts.

Rnd 18 *Sc in next st, sc2tog; rep from * around—12 sts.

Rnd 19 [Sc2tog] 6 times—6 sts. Fasten off leaving long tail.

Thread end in tapestry needle and weave through rem sts. Pull end to gather and fasten off securely.

BRIM

Rnd 1 (RS) With RS facing, join MC with a sc in any sc of bottom edge, then cont to sc in each st around—76 sts. *Do not join.* Mark last st made with the safety pin to indicate end of rnd.

Rnd 2 *Sc in next 3 sts, 2 sc in next st; rep from * around—95 sts.

Rnds 3–5 Sc in each st around.

Rnd 6 *Sc in next 4 sts, 2 sc in next st; rep from * around—114 sts.

Rnds 7–9 Sc in each st around.

Rnd 10 *Sc in next 5 sts, 2 sc in next st; rep from * around—133 sts.

Rnd 11 Sc in each st around. Fasten off.

Color wheel

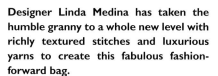

Designer Linda Medina has taken the humble granny to a whole new level with richly textured stitches and luxurious yarns to create this fabulous fashion-forward bag.

FINISHED MEASUREMENTS
▪ Approx 10"/25.5cm diameter x 2½"/6.5cm deep *(excluding handle)*

MATERIALS
▪ 1 1¾oz/50g ball (approx 100yd/91m) of Lane Borgosesia/Trendsetter Yarns *Merino Otto* (wool) in #11 black (A)

▪ 2 1¾oz/50g balls (each approx 100yd/91m) of Trendsetter Yarns *Tonalita* (wool/acrylic) in #2349 bright multi (B)

▪ 1 1¾oz/50g ball (approx 80yd/73m) of Trendsetter Yarns *Dune* (mohair/acrylic/nylon) in #58 teal/turquoise/purple (C)

▪ Size I/9 (5.5mm) crochet hook *or size to obtain gauge*
▪ ⅓ yd/.3m cotton lining fabric
▪ ⅝ yd/.6m black cotton fabric for under-lining
▪ ¾ yd/.75m fusible light-weight batting
▪ 22"/56cm length of ½"/13mm white cotton upholstery cording
▪ Magnetic purse snap
▪ Sewing needle and matching thread
▪ Four small safety pins

GAUGE
12 sts and 8 rnds to 4"/10cm over pat sts using size I/9 (5.5mm) crochet hook.
Take time to check gauge.

Note
To join yarn with a sc, make a slipknot and place on hook. Insert hook in st, yo, draw up a lp, yo and draw through both lps on hook.

STITCH GLOSSARY
PC (popcorn) Work 4 dc in same sp (or st). Remove loop from hook. Insert hook into top of first dc, then back into loop of last dc made. Draw loop through, then ch 1 to close popcorn.
BPC (beg popcorn) Ch 3 (counts as first dc of popcorn), work 3 dc in same sp. Remove loop from hook. Insert hook into 3rd ch of beg ch-3 top of first dc, then back into loop of last dc made. Draw loop through, then ch 1 to close popcorn.

BACK
With A, ch 4. Join ch with a sl st, forming a ring.
Rnd I (RS) Ch 1, 12 sc in ring, join rnd with a sl st in first st.
Rnd 2 Ch1, *sc in first st, 2 sc in next st; rep from * around, join rnd with a sl st in first st—18 sc. Fasten off.
Rnd 3 (RS) Join B with a sl st in same sp as joining, BPC in same sp, ch 3, *skip next sc, work PC, ch 3; rep from * around, join

rnd with a sl st in top of BPC—9 popcorns. Fasten off.

Rnd 4 (RS) Join C with a sl st in same sp as joining, ch 5 (counts as 1 dc and ch 2), *dc in top of next popcorn, ch 2, dc in next ch-3 sp, ch 2; rep from * around, join rnd with a sl st in 3rd ch of beg ch-5—18 dc and 18 ch-2 sps. Fasten off.

Rnd 5 (RS) Join B with a sl st in any ch-2 sp, ch 3 (counts as first dc), 2 dc in same sp, *skip next dc, 3 dc in next ch-2 sp; rep from * around, join rnd with a sl st in top of beg ch-3—54 dc. Fasten off.

Rnd 6 (RS) Join A with a sl st in same sp as joining, ch 1, sc in first and in each dc around, join rnd with a sl st in first sc—54 sc. Fasten off.

Rnd 7 (RS) Join B with a sl st in same sp as joining, BPC in same sp, ch 2, *skip next sc, work PC, ch 2; rep from * around, join rnd with a sl st in top of BPC—27 popcorns. Fasten off.

Rnd 8 (RS) Join C with a sl st in any ch-2 sp, ch 3 (counts as first dc), 2 dc in same sp, *skip next PC, 3 dc in next ch-2 sp; rep from * around, join rnd with a sl st in top of beg ch-3—81 dc. Fasten off.

Rnd 9 (RS) Join B with a sl st in same sp as joining, ch 1, sc in first and in each dc around, join rnd with a sl st in first sc—81 sc. Fasten off.

Rnd 10 (RS) Join C with a sl st in same sp as joining, ch 1, sc in first and in each sc

around, join rnd with a sl st in first sc—81 sc. Fasten off.

Work as for back.

With C, ch 62.

Row 1 (RS) Sc in 2nd ch from hook and in each ch across—61 sc. Turn.

Row 2 Ch 1, sc in each st across. Fasten off. Turn.

Row 3 Join A with a sc in first st, sc in each rem st across. Fasten off. *Do not turn.*

Row 4 Join B with a sl st in first st, ch 3 (counts as 1 dc), PC in next sc, *ch 2, skip next sc, PC in next sc; rep from *, end dc in last sc—30 popcorns. Fasten off. Turn.

Row 5 Join A with a sc in first dc, sc in top of each popcorn and in each ch-2 sp across, end with sc in top of beg ch-3—61 sc. Fasten off. Turn.

Row 6 Join C with a sc in first st, sc in each rem st across. Ch 1, turn.

Row 7 Sc in each st across. Fasten off.

Short side edging

Row 1 (RS) With RS facing and short side edge at top, join A with a sc in side edge of first row, work 8 more sc evenly spaced across. Fasten off. Rep on opposite short edge.

Joining

Place a safety pin to mark for beg of top

edge opening in any sc on last rnd of back. Count 27 sc from first marker and place a second safety pin marker in next sc to mark for end of top edge opening. Rep for front. With WS tog, pin long side edge of gusset to sides and bottom of back between markers—52 sts.

Rnd 1 (RS) With RS of back facing and working through both thicknesses, join B with a sc in next st after first marker, then sc in each st to 2nd marked st—52 sc. *Do not cut yarn.*

Cont along top edge of purse only as foll:

Top edging

Beg at marker, *sc in next 2 sts, 2 sc in next st; rep from * along top edge, end sc in next st, sc in last st with marker, join with a sl st to first sc of joining row. *Do not turn.*

Row 2 (RS) Ch 1, *working from left to right*, sc in each st across top edge only, join with a sl st to last sc of joining row. Fasten off.

Rep joining and top edging for front.

Handle

Row 1 (RS) From the RS, join A with a sc in first sc of short side edging of gusset, sc in next 8 sc. Turn.

Row 2 Ch 1, sc in each sc across. Turn. Rep row 2 until piece measures approx 20"/51cm from beg, end with a WS row.

Joining

Next row (RS) Hold last row of handle tog with opposite short side edging of gusset. Working through both thicknesses, sc in each st across. Fasten off.

FINISHING

Lining

Cut two 10½"/27cm circles and one 3½"/9cm wide x 21"/53cm long gusset from lining fabric. Cut two 10½"/27cm circles, one 3½"/9cm wide x 21"/53cm long gusset and one 2⅝"/7cm wide x 23"/58cm long cord cover from black underlining fabric. Cut two 9½"/24cm circles and one 2½"/8cm wide x 20"/51cm long gusset from batting. Measure and mark 2"/5cm from edge on RS of each lining fabric circle. Secure purse snap at marks following manufacturer's instructions.

Center and fuse batting circles to WS of lining circles. Place RS of lining and underlining circles together. Using ½"/1.3cm seam allowance throughout, sew together, beginning at edge opposite snap and leaving 3"/8cm opening for turning. Clip curves, turn, press and slip-stitch opening closed. Center and fuse batting gusset to WS of lining gusset. Place RS of lining and underlining gussets together. Sew together, beginning at center of a long side and leaving 3"/8cm opening for turning. Clip corners, turn, press and slip-stitch opening closed.

Fold each circle in half with snap at top of fold. Mark center bottom of folds with pin. Fold gusset in half, matching short edges, and mark center of each long edge with pin. With lining sides facing, match centers and pin circles to gusset. With thread doubled in needle, begin at center bottom and whipstitch gusset to one side of a circle. Beginning at center bottom, repeat for other side of same circle. Repeat for second circle.

Place lining in bag and slip-stitch underlining to first row worked of top edging. Do *not* stitch through lining. Do *not* sew gusset lining to bag gusset.

Handle

Press both long edges of cord cover $\frac{1}{2}$"/1.3cm to WS. Center cord on cover and whipstitch long edges together along folds. Tuck raw short edges to inside, covering cord ends, and whipstitch. Center covered cord on WS of handle and use A to whipstitch long edges of handle together. Use thread to slip-stitch inside handle ends to gusset underlining.

BABY BLANKET
Lullaby hues

Sweet dreams are made of this. Marianne Forrestal has designed a cuddly blankie just for baby using super-soft variegated yarn in soothing greens and lilacs.

FINISHED MEASUREMENTS
■ Approx 26"/66cm wide x 36"/91.5cm long

MATERIALS
■ 4 4oz/113g hanks (each approx 225yd/206m) of Lorna's Laces *Shepherd Worsted* (superwash wool) in #152 georgetown (4)
■ Size H/8 (5mm) crochet hook *or size to obtain gauge*

GAUGES
■ One small motif to 5"/12.5cm square using size H/8 (5mm) crochet hook.
■ 21½ sts and 9½ rws to 4"/10cm in dc/puff st pat using size H/8 (5mm) crochet hook.
Take time to check gauges.

SMALL MOTIF (MAKE 26)
Ch 6. Join ch with a sl st, forming a ring.

Rnd 1 (RS) Ch 5 (counts as 1 tr, ch 1), [tr in ring, ch 1] 15 times, join rnd with a sl st in 4th ch of beg ch-5.

Rnd 2 Sl st in first ch-1 sp, [yo, insert hook in same st, yo and draw up a loop] 3 times, yo and draw through all 7 loops on hook (puff st made), ch 2, *puff st in next ch-1 sp, ch 2; rep from * 14 times more, join rnd with a sl st in first puff st.

Rnd 3 Sl st in first ch-2 sp, ch 3 (counts as 1 dc), in same ch-sp work (2 dc, ch 1, 3 dc), ch 2, [sc in next ch-2 sp, ch 2] 3 times, *(3 dc, ch 1, 3 dc) in next ch-1 sp, ch 2, [sc in next ch-2 sp, ch 2] 3 times; rep from * twice more, join rnd with a sl st in top of beg ch-3.

Rnd 4 Sl st in next 2 dc and ch-1 sp, ch 3 (counts as 1 dc), in same ch-sp work (2 dc, ch 1, 3 dc), ch 1, [2 dc in next ch-2 sp, ch 1] 4 times, *(3 dc, ch 1, 3 dc) in next corner ch-1 sp, ch 1, [2 dc in next ch-2 sp, ch 1] 4 times, rep from * twice more, join rnd with a sl st in top of beg ch-3. Fasten off.

LARGE MOTIF
Work as for small motif through rnd 4. Do *not* fasten off.

Rnd 5 Sl st in next 2 dc and ch-1 sp, ch 3 (counts as 1 dc), in same ch-sp work (2 dc, ch 1, 3 dc), [ch 2, *puff st in next ch-1 sp, ch 2*; rep from * to * to next corner, (3 dc, ch 1, 3 dc) in corner ch-1 sp] 3 times, ch 2, rep from * to * to end, join rnd with a sl st in top of beg ch-3.

Rnd 6 Sl st in next 2 dc and ch-1 sp, ch 3 (counts as 1 dc), in same ch-sp work (2 dc, ch 1, 3 dc), [ch 1, *2 dc in next ch-2 sp, ch 1*; rep from * to * to next corner, (3 dc, ch 1, 3 dc) in corner ch-1 sp] 3 times, ch 1, rep from * to * to end, join rnd with a sl st in top of beg ch-3.

Rnds 7–18 Rep rnds 5 and 6 six times. Fasten off.

FINISHING

With RS tog and working in back loops only, whipstitch motifs tog foll assembly diagram.

Edging

Rnd I (RS) With RS facing, join yarn with a sl st in any corner ch-1 sp, ch 1, in same ch-sp work 3 sc, sc in each dc and ch-1 sp around, with 3 sc in each corner ch-1 sp, join rnd with a sl st in first sc.

Rnd 2 Ch 4, tr in same st as joining of rnd below, skip next 3 sc, sl st in next sc, *ch 4, tr in same sc as last sl st, skip next 3 sc, sl st in next sc; rep from * around, end last rep with sl st in same st as joining of rnd below. Fasten off.

Assembly Diagram

Large Motif

This fanciful medallion makes a delight-ful soft-sculpture necklace. Wear it on a leatherette cord to go casual or on a neck wire when you dress up. Designed by Lisa Pflug.

FINISHED MEASUREMENTS

◾ Approx 5"/12.5cm wide x 3"/7.5cm tall

MATERIALS

◾ 1 1¾oz/50g skein (approx 137yd/115m) of Rowan/Westminster Fibers, Inc. *Cotton Glace* (100% cotton) each in #814 shoot (A), #445 blood orange (B) and #749 sky (C) ③

◾ Size E/4 (3.5mm) crochet hook *or size to obtain gauge*

◾ 1yd/1m of narrow leatherette jewelry cord

◾ Two small safety pins

GAUGE

Motif is 2"/5cm square using size E/4 (3.5mm) crochet hook.
Take time to check gauge.

Note

To join yarn with a sc, make a slipknot and place on hook. Insert hook in ch-sp, yo, draw up a lp, yo and draw through both lps on hook.

MOTIF

To make an adjustable ring, with A, make a slipknot 10"/25.5cm from free end of yarn. Place slipknot on hook, then wrap free end of yarn twice around your first and second fingers on your left hand. Now work yarn coming from ball as follows:

Rnd 1 (RS) Ch 3 (counts as 1 dc), 2 dc in ring, [ch 2, 3 dc in ring] 3 times, ch 2, pull free end of yarn to close circle, then join rnd with a sl st in top of beg ch-3. Fasten off.

Rnd 2 (RS) Join B with a sl st in any ch-2 sp, ch 3 (counts as 1 dc), in same ch-sp work (2 dc, ch 2, 3 dc—beg corner made), ch 1, *(3 dc, ch 1, 3 dc) in next ch-1 sp, ch 1; rep from * around twice more, join rnd with a sl st in top of beg ch-3—4 corner ch-2 sps. Fasten off.

Rnd 3 (RS) Join C with a sc in any corner ch-2 sp, in same ch-sp work (2 sc, ch 1, 3 sc), ch 1, 3 sc in next ch-1 sp, ch 1, *(3 sc, ch 1, 3 sc) in next corner ch-2 sp, ch 1, 3 sc in next ch-1 sp, ch 1; rep from * around twice more, join rnd with a sl st in first sc. Fasten off.

Circles (make 2)

With C, make an adjustable ring. Work yarn coming from ball as follows:

Rnd 1 (RS) Ch 1, [sc, ch 1] 8 times in ring, pull free end of yarn to close circle, then join rnd with a sl st in first sc. Fasten off.

Rnd 2 (RS) Join B with a sc in any ch-1 sp, [ch 1, sc in next ch-1 sp] 7 times, ch 1, join rnd with a sl st in first sc. Do not fasten off.

Joining

With WS of motif and circle held tog, sl st in next sc of circle and center sc of any corner of motif. Fasten off. Make 2nd circle as for first, joining it to opposite corner of motif.

Hanging loops

With RS of motif facing, mark top of each circle (3 ch-1 sps from joining sl st) with a safety pin. Join A with a sl st in marked st of RH circle, ch 4, tr in center sc of 3-sc group on side edge of motif, ch 6, sl st in top of tr, ch 4, sl st in corner ch-1 sp at top corner of motif, [ch 6, sl st in same ch-sp] twice, ch 4, tr in center sc of 3-sc group on opposite side edge of motif, ch 6, sl st in top of tr, ch 4, sl st in mark st of LH circle. Fasten off. Thread cord through hanging loops. Cut cord to desired length.

Ring-a-ding-bling

Tiny bejeweled grannies make perfect fingerwear accessories for your fall or winter wardrobe. Designed by Shelby Allaho.

FINISHED MEASUREMENTS

■ Approx 1¼"/3cm square

MATERIALS

■ 1 1¾oz/50g ball (approx 92yd/85m) of Berroco, Inc. *Pure Merino* (extrafine merino wool) **❹**

Ring 1

■ 1 each in #8539 copper (A), #8573 nettle (B), #8527 resin (C) and #8560 bordeaux (D)

■ One 6mm round amber bead

■ Sixteen 11/0 ruby AB seed beads

■ Sixteen 3mm flat amber sequins

Ring 2

■ 1 each in #8560 bordeaux (A), #8542 kale (B) and #8553 mallard teal (C)

■ 1 .88oz/25g ball (approx 57yd/52m) of Berroco, Inc. *Jewel FX* (rayon/metallic) in #6910 alexandrites (D)

■ One 6mm round amethyst bead

■ Eight 11/0 sapphire AB seed beads

■ Eight 4mm flat aqua sequins

For both

■ Size G/6 (4mm) crochet hook *or size to obtain gauge*

■ Beading needle and invisible beading thread

GAUGE

Motif is 1¼"/3cm square using size G/6 (4mm) crochet hook.

Take time to check gauge.

MOTIF

With A, ch 6. Join ch with a sl st, forming a ring.

Rnd 1 (RS) Ch 3 (counts as 1 dc), 2 dc in ring, ch 3, [3 dc in ring, ch 3] 3 times, join rnd with a sl st in top of beg ch-3. Fasten off; set aside.

RING FRAME

With B, ch 6. Join ch with a sl st, forming a ring.

Rnd 1 (RS) [Ch 5, sl st in ring, sc in ring] 4 times, ch 10 (or as many ch needed to fit around your finger) sl st in the sc between the two ch-5 lps directly across from base of the ch-10 (this forms the ring band); work 12 sc over ring band (or as many sc needed to cover it), join with a sl st to frame. Fasten off.

First corner

With underside of ring frame facing, join C with a sl st in any ch-5 lp, *ch 2, 2 dc in same lp, sl st in same lp. Fasten off.*

Second corner

Working from left to right, join D for ring 1 (or one strand each of C and D held together for ring 2) in next ch-5 lp with a sl st. Rep from * to * as for first corner.

Third corner

Working from left to right, join C in next ch-5 lp with a sl st. Rep from * to * as for first corner.

Fourth corner

Work as for second corner.

With RS of motif facing and ring frame underneath, insert a corner through a ch-3 corner sp. Using B, and coming up through center hole of motif, embroider 3 straight stitches (one long stitch flanked by two shorter stitches) on each of the 4 sides.

Using beading needle and thread, sew 6mm bead to center of motif.

Adding beads and sequins

For each corner (for ring 2, omit beads and sequins on corners knit with C and D), sew 4 pairs of sequins and seed beads evenly spaced as foll: Bring needle up through corner. Thread on a sequin and a seed bead. Insert needle back through sequin and through to WS of corner. Cont to work in this manner until all sequins and beads have been sewn in place. Fasten off thread securely on WS.

Kaleidoscope

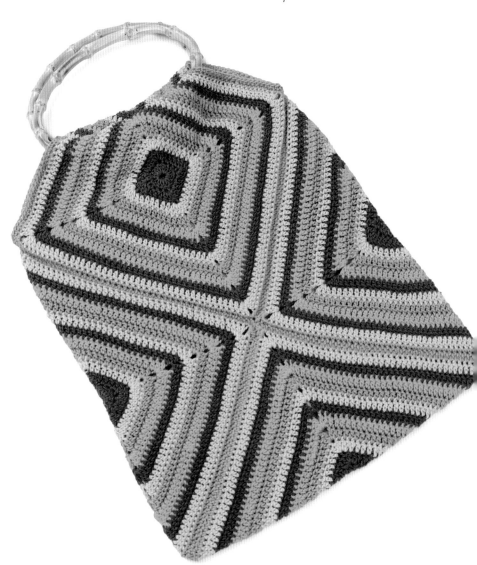

Four dazzling colorful squares seam together perfectly to create a roomy summer carryall. Designed by Diane Moyer.

FINISHED MEASUREMENTS

■ Approx 14"/35.5cm wide x 18"/45.5cm long *(excluding handles)*

MATERIALS

■ 2 1¾/50g hanks (each approx 110yd/100m) of Tahki Yarns/Tahki•Stacy Charles, Inc. *Cotton Classic* (mercerized cotton) each in #3912 red-violet (A), #3702 chartreuse (B), #3783 bright teal (C) and #3401 light bright orange (D) ▉4▉

■ Size 7 (4.5mm) crochet hook *or size to obtain gauges*

■ One pair 8¼"/21cm oval bamboo handles

■ ¾yd/.75m lining fabric

■ Sewing needle and matching thread

GAUGES

■ One motif to 11"/28cm square using size 7 (4.5mm) crochet hook.

■ 18 sts and 8¾ rnds to 4"/10cm over dc using size 7 (4.5mm) crochet hook.

Take time to check gauges.

MOTIF (MAKE 5)

With A, ch 5. Join ch with a sl st, forming a ring.

Rnd 1 (RS) Ch 3 (always counts as 1 dc), 15 dc in ring, join rnd with a sl st in top of beg ch-3—16 sts.

Rnd 2 Ch 3, 4 dc in same place as joining, dc in next 3 sts, *5 dc in next st, dc in next 3 sts; rep from * around, join rnd with a sl st in top of beg ch-3—4 5-dc corners made. Fasten off.

Rnd 3 (RS) Join B with a sl st in center st of any 5-dc corner, ch 3, 4 dc in same st as sl st, dc in next 7 sts, *5 dc in next st, dc in next 7 sts; rep from * around, join rnd with a sl st in top of beg ch-3. Fasten off.

Rnd 4 (RS) Join C with a sl st in center st of any 5-dc corner, ch 3, (dc, ch 2, 2 dc) in same st as sl st, dc in next 11 sts, *(2 dc, ch 2, 2 dc) in next st, dc in next 11 sts; rep from * around, join rnd with a sl st in top of beg ch-3—4 corner ch-2 sps. Fasten off.

Rnd 5 (RS) Join D with a sl st in any corner ch-2 sp, ch 3, (dc, ch 2, 2 dc) in same ch-sp, dc in next 15 sts, *(2 dc, ch 2, 2 dc) in next corner ch-2 sp, dc in next 15 sts; rep from * around, join rnd with a sl st in top of beg ch-3. Fasten off.

Rnd 6 (RS) Join A with a sl st in any corner ch-2 sp, ch 3, (dc, ch 2, 2 dc) in same ch-sp, dc in next 19 sts, *(2 dc, ch 2, 2 dc) in next corner ch-2 sp, dc in next 19 sts; rep from * around, join rnd with a sl st in top of beg ch-3. Fasten off.

Rnd 7 (RS) Join B with a sl st in any corner ch-2 sp, ch 3, (dc, ch 2, 2 dc) in same ch-sp, dc in next 23 sts, *(2 dc, ch 2, 2 dc) in next corner ch-2 sp, dc in next 23 sts; rep from * around, join rnd with a sl st in top of beg ch-3. Fasten off.

Rnd 8 (RS) Join C with a sl st in any corner ch-2 sp, ch 3, (dc, ch 2, 2 dc) in same ch-sp, dc in next 27 sts, *(2 dc, ch 2, 2 dc) in next corner ch-2 sp, dc in next 27 sts; rep from * around, join rnd with a sl st in top of beg ch-3. Fasten off.

Rnd 9 (RS) Join D with a sl st in any corner ch-2 sp, ch 3, (dc, ch 2, 2 dc) in same ch-sp, dc in next 31 sts, *(2 dc, ch 2, 2 dc) in next corner ch-2 sp, dc in next 31 sts; rep from * around, join rnd with a sl st in top of beg ch-3. Fasten off.

Rnd 10 (RS) Join A with a sl st in any corner ch-2 sp, ch 3, (dc, ch 2, 2 dc) in same ch-sp, dc in next 35 sts, *(2 dc, ch 2, 2 dc) in next corner ch-2 sp, dc in next 35 sts; rep from * around, join rnd with a sl st in top of beg ch-3. Fasten off.

Rnd 11 (RS) Join B with a sl st in any corner ch-2 sp, ch 3, (dc, ch 2, 2 dc) in same ch-sp, dc in next 39 sts, *(2 dc, ch 2, 2 dc) in next corner ch-2 sp, dc in next 39 sts; rep from * around, join rnd with a sl st in top of beg ch-3. Fasten off.

Rnd 12 (RS) Join C with a sl st in any corner ch-2 sp, ch 3, (dc, ch 2, 2 dc) in same ch-sp, dc in next 43 sts, *(2 dc, ch 2, 2 dc) in next corner ch-2 sp, dc in next 43 sts; rep from * around, join rnd with a sl st in top of beg ch-3. Fasten off.

Lightly block each square to measurements. With RS of 2 motifs facing, use C to sl st motifs tog across one edge, forming a strip. Working in the same manner, join 2 more motifs tog, then join the 2 strips, forming a square. With RS facing, lay large motif as in diagram A and fold 3 corners to meet in center. Use C and sl st edges tog, forming an envelope (see diagram B). With WS of last motif facing, insert so edges meet (see diagram C). Use C and sl st edges tog. Turn tote RS out.

Edging

With RS facing, join C with a sl st in st before any top corner.

Rnd 1 Ch 1, sc in same st as joining, sc in each st around top edge, working 3 sc in each corner st, join rnd with a sl st in first st. Fasten off. Lightly block seams.

Lining

Measure, mark and cut out two pieces of lining $1/2$"/1.3cm larger all around than tote. With RS tog and using a $1/2$"/1.3cm seam allowance, sew pieces together along straight side and bottom edges. Insert lining. Fold top edge of lining over to WS, so folded edge is $1/4$"/.5cm from edge of tote. Remove lining; press folded edges. Reinsert lining, then slip-stitch top edge of lining in place. Fold each top corner 4"/10cm over to WS, wrapping around a handle. Sew each corner securely in place.

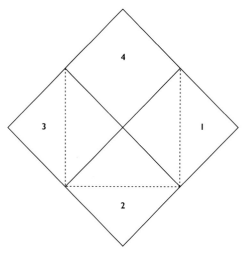

Diagram A

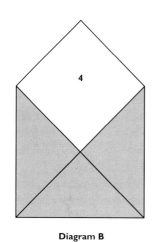

Diagram B

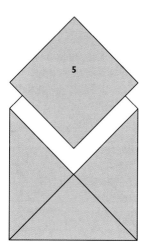

Diagram C

Sea-green dream

■■ ■■■ ■■■ ■■▶

Light, lacy and perfect for layering, Robyn Chachula's cropped topper spans the seasons. Wear with a tank top for warm-weather dressing or a turtleneck when the temperature drops.

Instructions are written for size Small. Changes for Medium, Large and X-Large are in parentheses.

FINISHED MEASUREMENTS

■ Bust (closed) 34 (38, 42½, 47½)"/86.5 (96.5, 108, 120.5)cm
■ Length 14¼" (15¾, 18½, 20½)"/36 (40, 47, 52)cm
■ Upper arm 12¾ (14¼, 17, 19)"/32.5 (36, 43, 48)cm

MATERIALS

■ 4 (4, 5, 5) 2½oz/70g hanks (each approx 150yd/137m) of Kolláge Yarns *Yummy* (bamboo/merino wool) in mala green (MC) ③
■ 2 hanks in milky green (CC)
■ Size H/8 (I/9, H/8, I/9)/5 (5.5, 5, 5.5)mm crochet hook *or size to obtain gauge*
■ 2 (2, 3, 3) 1⅛"/28mm buttons
■ 2 (2, 3, 3) size 4 sew-on snaps
■ 12"/30.5cm length of 1"/25mm matching grosgrain ribbon
■ Sewing needle and matching thread
■ Stitch markers

GAUGES

■ Whole motif to 4¼"/10.5cm square using H/8 (5mm) crochet hook.
■ Whole motif to 4¾"/12cm square using I/9 (5.5mm) crochet hook.
Take time to check gauges.

Notes

I Motif squares are joined on rnd 4 foll assembly diagram for size being made.
2 Read through entire instructions and refer to assembly diagram before beg to crochet.

STITCH GLOSSARY

CL (cluster st) In same sp [yo, insert hook into st, yo and draw up a lp, yo and draw through 2 lps on hook] 3 times, yo and draw through all 4 lps on hook.

dc2tog In same sp [yo, insert hook into st, yo and draw up a lp, yo and draw through 2 lps on hook] twice, yo and draw through all 3 lps on hook.

sc2tog [Insert hook in next st, yo and draw up a lp] twice, yo and draw through all 3 lps on hook.

WHOLE MOTIF [MAKE 16 (16, 33, 33)]

With size H/8 (I/9, H/8, I/9)/5 (5.5, 5, 5.5)mm hook and MC, ch 6. Join ch with a sl st, forming a ring.

Rnd I (RS) Ch 4 (counts as 1 dc, ch 1), [dc in ring, ch 1] 15 times, join rnd with a sl st in 3rd ch of beg ch-3—16 dc and ch-1 sps.

Rnd 2 Sl st in first ch-1 sp, ch 2 (counts as

1 dc), dc2tog in same ch-sp, ch 3, *CL in next ch-1 sp, ch 3; rep from * around, join rnd with a sl st in beg dc2tog.

Rnd 3 Sl st in first ch-3 sp, ch 1, sc in same ch-sp, *ch 5, sc in next ch-3 sp; rep from * around, end ch 2, dc in first sc.

Note: *Refer to joining and assembly diagrams before working rnd 4.*

Rnd 4 Ch 1, sc in joining dc of rnd below, *ch 5, sc in next ch-5 sp, (5 dc, ch 5, 5 dc) in next ch-5 sp, sc in next ch-5 sp, ch 5, sc in next ch-5 sp; rep from * around, end ch 5, sc in next ch-5 sp, (5 dc, ch 5, 5 dc) in next ch-5 sp, sc in last ch-5 sp, ch 5, join rnd with a sl st in first sc. Fasten off.

HALF MOTIF [MAKE 16 (16, 11, 11)]

With size H/8 (I/9, H/8, I/9)/5 (5.5, 5, 5.5)mm hook and MC, ch 6. Join ch with a sl st, forming a ring.

Row 1 (WS) Ch 3 (counts as a 1 dc), [dc in ring, ch 1] 7 times, 2 dc in ring—10 dc. Turn.

Row 2 Ch 2, dc in first dc, ch 3, *CL in next ch-1 sp, ch 3; rep from * 6 times more, end dc2tog in top of t-ch of row below. Turn.

Row 3 Ch 6 (counts as 1 tr and ch 2), sc in first ch-3 sp, *ch 5, sc in next ch- sp; rep from * 6 times more, end ch 2, tr in dc of row below. Turn.

Note: *Refer to joining and assembly diagrams before working row 4.*

Row 4 Ch 1, sc in tr, *ch 5, sc in next ch-5 sp, (5 dc, ch 5, 5 dc) in next ch-5 sp, sc in next ch-5 sp, ch 5, sc in next ch-5 sp; rep from * once more. Fasten off.

CURVED MOTIF [MAKE 2 (2, 0, 0)]

With size H/8 (I/9, H/8, I/9)/5 (5.5, 5, 5.5)mm hook and MC, ch 6. Join ch with a sl st, forming a ring.

Rnd 1 (RS) Ch 4 (counts as 1 dc, ch 1), [dc in ring, ch 1] 15 times, join rnd with a sl st in 3rd ch of beg ch-3—16 dc and ch-1 sps.

Rnd 2 Sl st in first ch-1 sp, ch 2 (counts as 1 dc), dc2tog in same ch-sp, ch 3, *CL in next ch-1 sp, ch 3; rep from * around, end CL in next ch-1 sp, ch 1, join rnd with a hdc in beg dc2tog. Turn. Work now in rows as foll:

Row 3 Ch 1, sc in hdc, [ch 5, sc in next ch-3 sp] 10 times, ch 2, dc in next ch-3 sp. Turn.

Note: *Refer to joining and assembly diagrams before working rnd 4.*

Rnd 4 Ch 1, sc in dc, *[ch 5, sc in next ch-5 sp] twice, (5 dc, ch 5, 5 dc) in next ch-5 sp, sc in next ch-5 sp, rep from *, end [ch 5, sc in next ch-5 sp] twice. Fasten off.

WEDGE MOTIF [MAKE 4 (4, 0, 0)]

With size H/8 (I/9, H/8, I/9)/5 (5.5, 5, 5.5)mm hook and MC, ch 21.

Row 1 (WS) Sc in 7th ch from hook, ch 5, skip next 3 ch, dc in next ch, ch 5, skip next 2 ch, dc in next ch, ch 5, skip next 3 ch, sc in next ch, ch 2, skip next 2 ch, sl st in last ch. Turn.

Row 2 Ch 1, sc in sl st, ch 5, sc in next ch-5 sp, (5 dc, ch 5, 5 dc) in next ch-5 sp, sc in next ch-5 sp, ch 5, skip (sc and 2 ch), sc in next ch of row below. Fasten off.

With size H/8 (I/9, H/8, I/9)/5 (5.5, 5, 5.5)mm hook and MC, ch 6. Join ch with a sl st, forming a ring.

Row 1 (WS) Ch 3 (counts as 1 dc), [dc in ring, ch 1] 11 times, 2 dc in ring—14 dc. Turn.

Row 2 Ch 2, dc in first dc, ch 3, *CL in next ch-1 sp, ch 3; rep from * 10 times more, end dc2tog in top of t-ch of row below. Turn.

Row 3 Ch 6 (counts as 1 tr and ch 2), sc in first ch-3 sp, *ch 5, sc in next ch-3 sp; rep from * 10 times more, end ch 2, tr in dc of row below. Turn.

Note: *Refer to joining and assembly diagrams before working row 4.*

Row 4 Ch 1, sc in tr, *ch 5, sc in next ch-5 sp, (5 dc, ch 5, 5 dc) in next ch-5 sp, sc in next ch-5 sp, ch 5, sc in next ch-5 sp; rep from * twice more. Fasten off.

With size H/8 (I/9, H/8, I/9)/5 (5.5, 5, 5.5)mm hook and MC, ch 6. Join ch with a sl st, forming a ring.

Rnd 1 (RS) Ch 4 (counts as 1 dc, ch 1), [dc in ring, ch 1] 15 times, join rnd with a sl st in 3rd ch of beg ch-3—16 dc and ch-1 sps.

Rnd 2 Sl st in first ch-1 sp, ch 2 (counts as 1 dc), dc2tog in same ch-sp, ch 3, *CL in next ch-1 sp, ch 3; rep from * around, CL in last ch-1 sp, ch 1, join rnd with a hdc in beg dc2tog. Turn. Work now in rows as foll:

Row 3 Ch 1, sc in hdc, [ch 5, sc in next ch-3 sp] 10 times, ch 2, dc in next ch-3 sp. Turn.

Note: *Refer to joining and assembly diagrams before working rnd 4.*

Rnd 4 Ch 1, sc in dc, *(5 dc, ch 5, 5 dc) in next ch-5 sp, sc in next ch-5 sp, [ch 5, sc in next ch-5 sp] twice; rep from * once more, end (5 dc, ch 5, 5 dc) in next ch-5 sp, sc in last ch-5 sp. Fasten off.

Two motifs

Refer to joining diagram and assembly diagram for size being made. Work rnd 4 to first (5 dc, ch 5, 5 dc) corner, instead work 5 dc in next ch-5 sp, ch 2, sl st to adjacent motif's corner ch-5 sp, ch 2, 5 dc in same ch-5 sp, [sc in next ch-5 sp, ch 2, sl st to adjacent motif's ch-5 sp edge, ch 2] twice, sc in next ch-5 sp, 5 dc in next ch-5 sp, ch 2, sl st to adjacent motif's corner ch-5 sp, ch 2, 5 dc in same ch-5 sp, cont to work rnd 4 to the end.

Joining more motifs

Foll instructions for each motif. Join all corner ch-5 sps and edges with a sl st instead of the center ch. Join all motifs foll assembly diagram.

FINISHING

Block to measurements. Fold piece in half, then join motifs at side and sleeve edges as before.

Outer edging

With RS facing and size H/8 (I/9, H/8, I/9)/5 (5.5, 5, 5.5)mm hook, join CC with a sl st in left side seam.

Rnd 1 (RS) Ch 1, sc evenly along edge of half motif to end, *ch 2, sc evenly along edge of next half motif; rep from * for half, wedge, curved and corner motifs. For whole motifs, work as foll: **2 sc in corner ch-5 sp, ch 4, 3 sc in edge ch-5 sp, ch 2, 3 sc in edge ch-5 sp, ch 4, 2 sc in corner ch-5 sp corner; rep from ** along all whole motifs. Cont to work in this manner around entire outer edge, join rnd with a sl st in first sc.

Place 16 (16, 18, 18) stitch markers evenly spaced around bottom edge of body, 3 markers evenly spaced along back neck edge, one marker centered on each shoulder, then one marker in each corner of front neck.

Rnd 2 Ch 1, *sc in each st to marker, sc2tog; rep from * around, join rnd with a sl st in first sc.

Rnds 3–5 Ch 1, *sc in each st to next sc2tog of rnd below, sc2tog over sc2tog and next st, rep from * around, join rnd with a sl st in first sc.

Rnds 6 and 7 Ch 1, sc in each st around, join rnd with a sl st in fist sc. When rnd 7 is completed, fasten off.

Sleeve edging

With RS facing and size H/8 (I/9, H/8, I/9)/5 (5.5, 5, 5.5)mm hook, join CC with a sl st in sleeve seam.

Rnd 1 (RS) Ch 1, sc evenly along edge of first motif, *ch 2, sc evenly along edge of next motif; rep from * around, join rnd with a sl st in first sc.

Place 6 (6, 8, 8) stitch markers evenly spaced around sleeve.

Rnd 2 Ch 1, *sc in each st to stitch marker, sc2tog; rep from * around, join rnd with a sl st in first sc.

Rnds 3 and 4 Ch 1, *sc in each st to sc2tog of rnd below, sc2tog over sc2tog and next st; rep from * around, join rnd with a sl st in first sc.

Rnd 5 Ch 1, sc in each st around, join rnd with a sl st to first sc. Fasten off.

Block edgings. Cut grosgrain ribbon into six 2"/5cm pieces. Fold cut edges ½"/1.3cm to WS and sew in place for ribbon tabs. Try on top. Place markers for top halves of 2 snaps on WS of right front edging, spacing them 2"/5cm apart. Place markers for bottom halves to correspond on RS of left front. On WS of right front edging, place a ribbon tab over first marker, then place top half of snap on top. Sew snap in place, going through all layers. Working in the same manner, sew on 2nd snap top, corresponding bottoms, then rem snap where front neck edges overlap. Sew on buttons using CC.

Joining Diagram

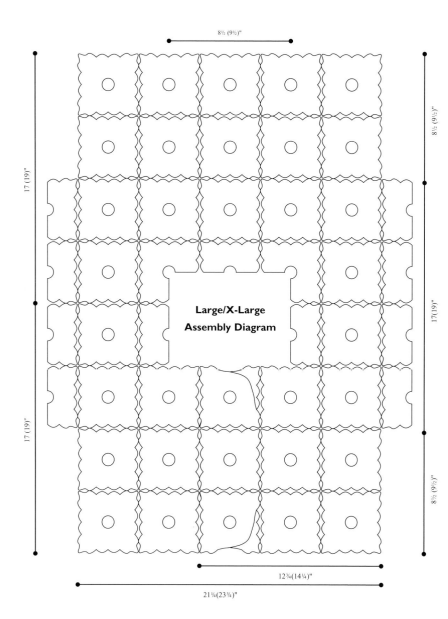

8½ (9½)"

8½ (9½)"

17 (19)"

17(19)"

17 (19)"

8½ (9½)"

Large/X-Large
Assembly Diagram

12¾(14¼)"

21¼(23¾)"

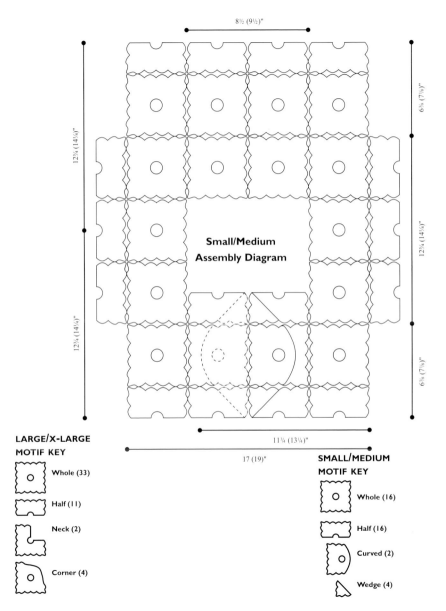

8½ (9½)"

6⅜ (7⅛)"

12¾ (14¼)"

12¾ (14¼)"

12¾ (14¼)"

6⅜ (7⅛)"

Small/Medium Assembly Diagram

11¾ (13¼)"

17 (19)"

LARGE/X-LARGE MOTIF KEY

Whole (33)

Half (11)

Neck (2)

Corner (4)

SMALL/MEDIUM MOTIF KEY

Whole (16)

Half (16)

Curved (2)

Wedge (4)

AMISH AFGHAN

Raise the barn

Michele Maks Thompson has duplicated the look of the classic sunshine-and-shadow quilt pattern in crochet using a handsome array of traditional colors.

FINISHED MEASUREMENTS

▨ Approx 55½"/141cm wide x 55½"/141cm long

MATERIALS

▨ 3 3½oz/100g skeins (each approx 166yd/152m) of Moda Dea/Coats & Clark *Washable Wool* (superwash merino wool) each in #4491 rust (B), #4477 claret (C) and #4465 coffee (F) (**4**)

▨ 2 skeins each in #4461 maize (A), #4435 taupe (D), #4441 lake blue (E) and #4440 moss (G)

▨ Sizes H/8 and I/9 (5 and 5.5mm) crochet hooks *or sizes to obtain gauges*

GAUGES

▨ 4 rnds to 5"/12.5cm over dc motif using size I/9 (5.5mm) crochet hook.

▨ 11 sts and 6 rows to 3"/7.5cm over dc border using size I/9 (5.5mm) crochet hook. *Take time to check gauges.*

COLOR SEQUENCE

*2 rnds (or rows) each A, B, C, D, E, F, G; rep from * for color sequence.

CENTER MOTIF

With larger hook and A, ch 3. Join ch with a sl st, forming a ring.

Rnd 1 (RS) Ch 3 (counts as 1 dc), 2 dc in ring, ch 3, [3 dc in ring, ch 3] 3 times, join rnd with a sl st in top of beg ch-3—4 corner ch-3 sps.

Rnd 2 Sl st to first corner ch-3 sp, ch 3 (counts as 1 dc), in same ch-sp work (2 dc, ch 3, 3 dc—beg corner made), ch 1, *(3 dc, ch 3, 3 dc) in next ch-3 sp, ch 1; rep from * around twice more, join rnd with a sl st in top of beg ch-3. Fasten off.

Rnd 3 (RS) Join B with a sl st in any corner ch-3 sp, ch 3, in same ch-sp work (2 dc, ch 3, 3 dc), ch 1, 3 dc in next ch-1 sp, ch 1, *(3 dc, ch 3, 3 dc) in next corner ch-3 sp, ch 1, 3 dc in next ch-1 sp, ch 1; rep from * around twice more, join rnd with a sl st in top of beg ch-3.

Rnd 4 Sl st to first corner ch-3 sp, ch 3, in same ch-sp work (2 dc, ch 3, 3 dc), ch 1, [3 dc in next ch-1 sp, ch 1] twice, *(3 dc, ch 3, 3 dc) in next corner ch-1 sp, ch 1, [3 dc in next ch-1 sp, ch 1] twice; rep from * around twice more, join rnd with a sl st in top of beg ch-3. Fasten off.

Rnd 5 (RS) Join C with a sl st in any corner ch-3 sp, ch 3, in same ch-sp work (2 dc, ch 3, 3 dc), ch 1, [3 dc in next ch-1 sp, ch 1] 3 times, *(3 dc, ch 3, 3 dc) in next corner ch-1 sp, ch 1, [3 dc in next ch-1 sp, ch 1] 3 times; rep from * around twice more, join rnd with a sl st in top of beg ch-3.

Rnd 6 Sl st to first corner ch-3 sp, ch 3, in same ch-sp work (2 dc, ch 3, 3 dc), ch 1, [3 dc in next ch-1 sp, ch 1] 4 times, *(3 dc, ch

3, 3 dc) in next corner ch-1 sp, ch 1, [3 dc in next ch-1 sp, ch 1] 4 times; rep from * around twice more, join rnd with a sl st in top of beg ch-3. Fasten off.

Rnd 7 (RS) Join D with a sl st in any corner ch-3 sp, ch 3, in same ch-sp work (2 dc, ch 3, 3 dc), ch 1, [3 dc in next ch-1 sp, ch 1] 5 times, *(3 dc, ch 3, 3 dc) in next corner ch-1 sp, ch 1, [3 dc in next ch-1 sp, ch 1] 5 times; rep from * around twice more, join rnd with a sl st in top of beg ch-3.

Rnd 8 Sl st to first corner ch-3 sp, ch 3, in same ch-sp work (2 dc, ch 3, 3 dc), ch 1, [3 dc in next ch-1 sp, ch 1] 6 times, *(3 dc, ch 3, 3 dc) in next corner ch-1 sp, ch 1, [3 dc in next ch-1 sp, ch 1] 6 times; rep from * around twice more, join rnd with a sl st in top of beg ch-3. Fasten off.

Rnds 9–30 Working in color sequence as established, cont to change colors every other rnd and work one more 3-dc group between corners every rnd.

Corner

Row 1 (RS) With larger hook, join B with a sl st in corner ch-3 sp, ch 4, *skip next 3-dc group, 3 dc in next ch-1 sp, ch 1, rep from * to next corner ch-3 sp, dc in corner ch-3 sp—2 3-dc groups dec. Turn.

Row 2 Ch 4, *skip next 3-dc group, 3 dc in next ch-1 sp, ch 1, rep from * to beg ch-4 sp of row below, dc in ch-4 sp—2 3-dc groups dec. Fasten off. Turn.

Row 3 Join C with a sl st around ending dc of row below, ch 4, *skip next 3-dc group, 3 dc in next ch-1 sp, ch 1, rep from * to ch-4 sp of row below, dc in ch-4 sp. Turn.

Row 4 Ch 4, *skip next 3-dc group, 3 dc in next ch-1 sp, ch 1, rep from * to ch-4 sp of row below, ch 1, dc in ch-4 sp. Fasten off. Turn.

Working in color sequence as established, cont to change colors every other row and decrease two 3-dc groups *every* row until only one 3-dc group rem, end with a RS row. Turn.

Last row Ch 3, skip first dc, dc in next dc, skip last dc, dc in ch-4 sp. Fasten off.

Rep for 3 rem corners.

Border

Row 1 (RS) With larger hook, join B with a sl st in center dc of last row of corner, ch 3, 3 dc in each ch-sp across, end dc in center dc of last row of opposite corner. Turn.

Rows 2–6 Ch 3, dc in each st across. Turn. When row 6 is completed, fasten off.

Rep border with B on opposite side edge.

Rep border with C on 2 rem side edges.

CORNER MOTIFS (MAKE 4)

With larger hook and E, ch 3. Join ch with a sl st, forming a ring.

Rnds 1 and 2 Rep rnds 1 and 2 of center motif.

Rnd 3 Sl st to first corner ch-3 sp, ch 1, 5 sc

in same ch-sp, sc in each st and ch-1 sp around, working 5 sc in each corner ch-3 sp, join rnd with a sl st, in first sc. Fasten off.

FINISHING
Whipstitch corner motifs to border, using colors to match.

Edging

Rnd 1 (RS) With smaller hook and F, join yarn with a sl st in any st along side edge, ch 1, sc in each st around and 3 sc in center sc of each corner, join rnd with a sl st in first st.

Rnds 2 and 3 Ch 1, sc in each sc around and 3 sc in center sc of each corner, join rnd with a sl st in first st. When rnd 3 is completed, fasten off.

RESOURCES

U.S. RESOURCES

Write to the yarn companies listed below for purchasing and mail-order information.

Berroco, Inc.
P.O. Box 367
14 Elmdale Road
Uxbridge, MA 01569
www.berroco.com

Caron International
P.O. Box 222
Washington, NC 27889
www.caron.com

Coats & Clark
P.O. Box 12229
Greenville, SC 29612
www.coatsandclark.com

Colinette
distributed by
Unique Kolours, Ltd.
www.colinette.com

Dale of Norway
4750 Shelburne Road
Shelburne, VT 05482
www.dale.no

Knit One, Crochet Too, Inc.
91 Tandberg Trail, Unit 6
Windham, ME 04062
www.knitonecrochettoo.com

Knitting Fever, Inc. (KFI)
P.O. Box 336
315 Bayview Avenue
Amityville, NY 11701
www.knittingfever.com

Kolláge Yarns
3304 Blue Bell Lane
Birmingham, AL 35242
www.kollageyarns.com

Lane Borgosesia
distributed by
Trendsetter Yarns

Lion Brand Yarn
34 West 15th Street
New York, NY 10011
www.lionbrand.com

Lorna's Laces
4229 North Honore Street
Chicago, IL 60613
www.lornaslaces.net

Louet North America
808 Commerce Park Drive
Ogdensburg, NY 13669
www.louet.com

Moda Dea
distributed by
Coats & Clark
www.modadea.com

Nashua Handknits
distributed by
Westminster Fibers, Inc.

Noro
distributed by
KFI

Plymouth Yarn Co.
P.O. Box 28
Bristol, PA 19007
www.plymouthyarn.com

Rowan
distributed by
Westminster Fibers, Inc.
www.knitrowan.com

Tahki•Stacy Charles, Inc.
70-30 80th Street,
Building 36
Ridgewood, NY 11385
www.tahkistacycharles.com

Tahki Yarns
distributed by
Tahki•Stacy Charles, Inc.

Trendsetter Yarns
16745 Saticoy Street,
Suite #101
Van Nuys, CA 91406
www.trendsetteryarns.com

Unique Kolours, Ltd.
28 N. Bacton Hill Road
Malvern, PA 19355
www.uniquekolours.com

Westminster Fibers, Inc.
4 Townsend Avenue, Unit 8
Nashua, NH 03063
www.westminsterfibers.com

CANADIAN RESOURCES

Write to U.S. resources for mail-order availability of yarns not listed.

Louet North America
R.R. 4
Prescott, Ontario
Canada K0E 1T0
www.louet.com

The Old Mill Knitting Co.
P.O. Box 81176
Ancaster, Ontario
Canada L9G 4X2
www.oldmillknitting.com

Trendsetter Yarns
distributed by
The Old Mill Knitting Co.

U.K. RESOURCES

Write to U.S. resources for mail-order availability of yarns not listed.

Rowan
Green Lane Mill
Holmfirth, England HD9 2DX
United Kingdom
www.knitrowan.com

GRANNIES ON THE GO!

Editorial Director
ELAINE SILVERSTEIN

Executive Editor
CARLA S. SCOTT

Book Division Manager
ERICA SMITH

Senior Editor
MICHELLE BREDESON

Art Director
DIANE LAMPHRON

Associate Art Director
SHEENA T. PAUL

Yarn Editor
TANIS GRAY

Instructions Editors
PAT HARSTE
JEANNIE CHIN

Photography
JACK DEUTSCH STUDIO

Copy Editor
KRISTINA SIGLER

Vice President, Publisher
TRISHA MALCOLM

Production Manager
DAVID JOINNIDES

Creative Director
JOE VIOR

President
ART JOINNIDES

■

LOOK FOR THESE OTHER TITLES IN THE ON THE GO! SERIES...

■